Private Lives in the Imperial City

Private Lives
in the
Imperial City

John Leonard

Alfred A. Knopf   New York • 1979

THIS IS A BORZOI BOOK
PUBLISHED BY ALFRED A. KNOPF, INC.

All of these pieces originally appeared in slightly different form in *The New York Times*.

Library of Congress Cataloging in Publication Data
Leonard John. Private lives in the imperial city.
I. Title.
PS3562.E56P7 1979   814.'5'4   78-20559
ISBN 0-394-50170-5

Manufactured in the United States of America
First Edition

This book belongs to Andrew and Amy
(and to Jennifer, who came later),

with special thanks to Arthur Gelb,
whose idea the whole thing was.

Contents

Next   3

The Leak   6

Gifts   9

Cheevered   12

Good News   15

Plastic   18

Bowling   21

The Imperial City   24

New York Women   27

About Cats (I)   30

Oliver   33

Youth   36

The Pampas   39

On Being Stupid   42

On Being Excellent   45

On Being Average   48

Tinkertoys   51

The Stoop   54

Baseball   57

The Power Party   60

Communities   63

The Support System   66

Suckers   69

Contents

Sir, I Exist   72

The Garden of Schopenhauer   75

Questions and Answers   78

The Sweet Science   81

My Son, the Roman   84

Crazy in the Kitchen   87

Red Rover   90

The Only Child   93

When Naiads Meet Raccoons   96

Father Bird   99

Rainbowed   102

About Cats (II)   105

Perfect Knowledge in Final Things   108

The Australians in Paris   111

The Nightcap   114

The Afghan   117

Love   120

Water Games   123

Don't Tell My Friends   126

Three Truths   129

Faces   132

Snapshots   135

On Being Embarrassed   138

White Tigers   141

Dash   144

Interior Monologue   147

Among the Poets   150

Deductible Me   153

ix

A Victim of Surprises 156

Spinoza and Pork Chops 159

To Dance or Not to Dance 162

The Permanent Relationship 165

Civility 168

Downwardly Mobile 171

Pregnant 174

The Burning Question 177

The Ear 180

Everybody Is Wrong 183

Not Quite 186

California in Rochester 189

On Honor 192

The Diet 195

Going to Greece 198

Dolphins 201

It and Who 204

The Caryatid 207

Private Lives in the Imperial City

Next

You are thirty-seven years old, which, according to Aristotle, is the ideal age for a man to marry. And so you have decided to marry, for the second time. It is odd how much morbid interest such a decision excites in a city otherwise prepared to tolerate almost any bizarre relationship among animals, vegetables and minerals. Marry? Again? How quaint! What for? Friends walk around your behavior, poke at it with a stick; take snapshots, as though they were anthropologists happening upon a Druid or the Ik.

If those friends are full of literary vapors, they will quote Dr. Johnson on second marriages: "The triumph of hope over experience." Or Sheridan: "Zounds! madam, you had no taste when you married me!" Or Ambrose Bierce:

> *They stood before the altar and supplied*
> *The fire themselves in which their fat was fried.*

To which you may want to reply with a Dutch proverb: In marrying and taking pills it is best not to think about it too much.

But of course you have thought of little else as you've gone about your rounds of finding a ring, and finding a doctor who will bleed you and sign a bill of adequate health; and finding a clerk at City Hall who will sell you permission; and finding a judge who will come to your home and who will agree not to quote Kahlil Gibran in the service.

There are reasons of state for marrying a second time, instead of persisting in relationships (which are to marriage what gum is to nutrition): income tax returns, life insurance, health insurance, passports, joint checking accounts, custody of Bloomingdale's, all those slips of paper, cards of identity, by whose arithmetic one adds up to a personality in the modern world. Let's keep it simple for the computers.

There are, moreover, two sets of children to consider. It would be better for them at school if, on explaining their domestic arrangements, they didn't sound like innocent bystanders in a particularly messy covert operation of the Cold War. Perhaps you think they would prefer to be elsewhere on the appointed Saturday. Don't let them be anywhere else. A son shouldn't go to the movies while his father is being married. If they stand around variously impersonating bookends, alarm clocks, ghosts, sentries, tourists or refugees, give them a poem to read or some flowers to hold. They are important witnesses. It isn't necessary that they altogether understand you; it is necessary that they take you seriously.

Whereas, bubonic plague wouldn't keep the two sets of parents, yours and hers, away from this occasion. They couldn't care less whether you are going through a mid-life "crisis" or a mid-life "passage"—so long as you're married. They will fly in from Bangkok or Reykjavik, to dust the furniture and hope for the best. They have been through these revolving doors before; you might even have attended one or two of *their* weddings. Let's keep doing it until we get it right. Along with the wheels of cheese and potted plants, wads of tissue and baby pictures, they will bring you a blank check on their loyalty.

As for your friends—those strangers, like your second wife, that you have taken into your house without the advice and consent of your parents—they will as usual finish off your Scotch, steal your books, burn holes in your patience, and make you laugh. They tiptoe up and down the stairs because, on the next landing or just coming out of a closet, there might be an ex-husband or an ex-wife or, for that matter, the Sullivanian analyst on the West Side to whom half of them had gone when they were sad. How unlike the first time, when we were all promising, confident, stupid, graduate students of ourselves, unblotched copybooks. Your friends now are halfway through the novels of their lives, and worried about the next couple of chapters. And yet, after all the jokes, they are genuinely happy for you, for the surprise twist in your plot. Weddings are nice; maybe it's part of the nostalgia craze.

That first time, everything was supposed to be grand. Someone had wanted to roast an ox on a spit in a pit of coals, and for there to be bagpipes in the apple trees and fox-trotting under the great elms and an acre of sunlight like a shield reflecting off the wine-glass and the brass buttons of the blue blazers, as though we were advising Mars by semaphore of our golden youth.

Not so on a November Saturday in the city of New York in 1976. No bagpipes. Maybe a harpsichord or a guitar. Casual clothes. Scraps of Donne and Yeats:

> But let a gentle silence wrought with music flow
> Whither her footsteps go.

Is this a caution? Having domesticated the beasts of pride, does one these days walk one's luck warily around the block on a leash, instead of bragging about it? Is it safer to settle for what W. S. Gilbert called a "modified rapture"?

No. Having earned your modesty, this time be careful. You marry, not for reasons of state or children or parents or friends, but for yourself and the one you love, in gratitude. You are setting up a sanctuary, and know that it is fragile. You hope that you are finally a serious character in your own life, that everyone will be-lieve this time you are and will behave like an adult, instead of one of those toys on the streets with the keys sticking out of their pineal glands, doing mindless damage. To quote Yeats again:

> How but in custom and ceremony
> Are innocence and beauty born?

You marry to be worthy of a gift, and want to say so out loud, but without shouting. One doesn't shout a prayer. Marriage is one of the few ceremonies left to us about which it is impossible—or at least self-demeaning—to be cynical. Then, in secret, rejoice.

The Leak

It happened the first cold Saturday night in his new house. Or, rather, he was new and the house was old, more than a hundred years old, a brownstone fixed up inside to look like autumn leaves. And he hadn't known that Saturday was especially cold because, along with the woman of the house and a pair of friends rented for the evening, he had been sitting in front of the fireplace burning money. Not real money, of course, but one of those chemical slabs, compounds of sawdust and wax and coloring agents and wrapping paper, for which New Yorkers pay quite a bit of real money in order to pretend for two hours that they are burning a cedar log in a fireplace the size of a qualm.

The children were asleep. The adults, as they would have described themselves, had been discussing whatever New Yorkers discuss at such times—Amy Carter and public schools, Sufi mysticism, petrodollars, the anguish of the Third Dimension—and by midnight it was clear they had reached an adjournment of minds. The friends departed. The woman of the house went to bed. He would gather up the coffee cups and turn off the lights and bar the doors. It was then he discovered that there was no heat; every radiator in the house was cold and silent.

Going to the cellar seemed a sensible idea. Like most cellars, it was full of parts of his life he no longer knew what to do with, cardboard boxes of old emotions. It was also, alas, full of water, a two-inch carpet of water on the cellar floor, and a gurgling, as of blood, in the darkness. Removing shoes and socks, he waded in. The furnace throbbed. By following an overhead pipe from the furnace, he arrived at the source of the water. A valve, cleverly positioned out of his reach, had no apparent purpose other than to gush water on his floor, water that should have gone to the radiators, condensing into steam instead of causing mud.

On a rickety chair, he attacked the valve. It wouldn't budge.

Up, again, then, the stairs to what was known, preposterously, as the tool drawer. Like too many New Yorkers, he bought tools one at a time, each for a specific disaster; the drawer was an anthology of these disasters. Nothing availed. The valve, standing by the water, would not be moved.

Equally unavailing was a visit to the Yellow Pages. (There are no all-night plumbers at one o'clock on a Sunday morning in Manhattan. There are only answering machines. Perhaps the machines talk to one another. The night seemed filled with their squawks and beeps, a kind of whale music in the cavities of the teeth.) He thought of draining the water by garden hose through the cellar window, but that would mean his standing up all night on the chair with a funnel clapped over the valve and the hose coiled about his shoulders like a boa constrictor.

Nor, when he hit upon emptying the two big green plastic garbage bins—thus filling the front hall with trash—could he get the hose to work as a siphon. The hose was too long and his breath too short. There was nothing to do but to watch each bin fill up with water, substitute the empty bin for the full one, and try to slop the contents of the full one down the cellar sink, which of course was tiny and clogged.

He should have awakened his fourteen-year-old son to help, but that would mean looking like a jerk in front of his son. And so he sat on the wooden cellar steps, barefoot, nipping brandy, waiting for the dawn, a brooder:

"Accustomed as I am to dark nights of the soul, this is the first one that's sprung a leak. Maybe I should turn off the furnace. But I don't know how. Why is it I so seldom know how? Even as a child, I never saw anything in the microscope and my model airplanes looked like birds' nests. Buying a house was a grave error; it doesn't come with a landlord or a super or a handyman, people to blame. To my friends, it may look like autumn leaves. To me, it is a rainbow of debt."

But he had bought the house to declare his adulthood. His family would no longer be transients, refugees. Mortgages were a form of seriousness. Having sought to expand his protection, had he merely multiplied occasions for incompetence? His children supposed him capable of heroism. What if they found out he couldn't shut a valve, wire a lamp, speak French, read music, solve differential equations, remember to buy flowers, explain seizures of melancholy? What, in fact, *could* he do?

He could make money, fry bacon, wiggle his ears, get to airports on time, read Latin-American novels all the way through, know what happened the previous night in every professional sport, take children seriously, be fair except when it hurt his own feelings, sing tenor and quote Swinburne. Somehow, this didn't add up to much. Where was the manliness? He loathed hunting and fishing, had never been a warrior, didn't dream of sports cars. He resembled a real American father as much as those chemical logs resembled real cedar: a facsimile of wax and sawdust. Would Noah have waited barefoot for a plumber?

Just as he was thinking that adulthood itself is a myth, that we are all of us statistical inferences from credit cards and insurance policies and income tax returns and traffic tickets, there came a voice:

"Dad? What's all the trash doing in the front hall?"

His son—with whom he wanted to discuss the poetry of science, the black hole and the double helix; for whom he would lay down his wallet and his life; this excellence—would want reasons and breakfast.

"Dad," said his son, "this is a joke I made up. What's your name?"

Numbly, he told his son his name.

"WRONG!" screamed his son. And laughed as if with hernia. "You get it, Dad? It really upsets people when you tell them they're *wrong* about their own names. That's the only thing they're sure of."

The valve? The valve, according to the eventual plumber, was there to protect the house from an overload of water in the pipes. Because of a faulty furnace switch, there had been an overload on Saturday night. If he had managed to shut the valve, his Ark would have exploded.

Gifts

She is ten years old. She has just asked: "What do you want for Christmas?" What you want for Christmas, of course, is that she remain ten years old, forever, with her skin the color of clean sand and her fierce will—the ticking of the blue vein at her temple as though the brain were an alarm clock; her avidity and her perfect assurance that the people in the next room, the tall strangers, will find her of compelling interest; her sense of justice and the way she opens cans of soup. Or, if she insists on growing up, you want her to be a marine biologist or President of the United States.

"Why don't you make me something?" is your reply.

This is received with a sigh the size of Ken Russell's effrontery. "Damn it," she says. (Your daughter isn't perfect: she talks on occasion like a guttersnipe and watches reruns of *Gilligan's Island*.) It seems that she has saved up twenty-three dollars, and yet her mother, her grandmother, her grandfather and her uncle all want her to make something for them. "Why can't we have an old-fashioned Christmas where you buy things?"

Fathers specialize in not being able to answer the important questions. And you are especially ill equipped to explain the metaphysics of gift-giving, the erotics of buying, the politics of consumption. You have always found the exchange of gifts to be somehow sinister, a bartering of psychic yard goods and symbolic energies. You don't think of yourself as a consumer, except of alcohol; in a nation of mouths, you are an ear or a thumb. Department stores remind you of hospitals and prison camps.

Why is this? Why the anxiety at Christmas and birthdays, those orgies of disappointment, of boxes disemboweled, of wrapping paper like bandages pulled off emotions? Why, ever since you were your daughter's age and got a Kodak Brownie camera, haven't you been happy on December 25th? It's not that you're some lofty anchorite, a soul beyond the veil of Maya, a tune whistled at midnight in a Himalayan comfort station. The rooms of your life are upholstered. You have chosen thousands of books. You brood in an Eames chair. You are surrounded by what a French Existentialist called "objects opaque in their servitude." You dream of an ice-cube machine. You will end with a Pacemaker.

Of the various holidays about which one is supposed to be enthusiastic, you most approve Thanksgiving. Gifts aren't involved. Food disappears. There is so much food, as a matter of fact, that it isn't necessary to eat; no one is watching but the pumpkin pie. Poems or prayers are composed with ball-point drumsticks. Friends lie down on a bed of stuffing. If the children are bored, they can watch football or make Christmas presents.

You approve, too, of your friends. They sat there last Thursday like history taking the afternoon off, variously heroic in their marriages and work, made longer by their stretch on the water wheel of time, desiring to please. You noticed that they drank less and smoked less than New Yorkers used to. You observed that your son had formed his first crush on a member of the opposite sex, and his taste impressed you. You listened to conversation about the strategy of the bite in vampire movies. You thought to ask about the psychology of gifts, the ambiguity of purchase, the trauma of receivership, the suction of reciprocity. Your friends are hard to interrupt, but appreciate you as a consumer of other people's ideas.

And it was the idea of giving that they plucked and strummed, like a turkey or a hang-up. A gift, after all, is somebody else's idea of who you are, a guess. You may not know what you want or need—that may be your problem: "Moyst, with one drop of thy blood, my drye soul!" Donne asked Christ—and be surprised when you get it. You may be appalled to learn, from their gifts, what other people think of you. Have they so radically misperceived? Have I so deliberately misrepresented? Do they know me so little, or too well? Can I abide their estimate? And do you, on giving, dare to define your feelings for another, the limits of your apprehension?

On hearing all this, you had minced emotions. Inside every

gift box is an intimacy and a time bomb, a presumption and a curse. You give, most of the time, books and long-playing records, stating your spiritual whereabouts when doing so, assuming the recipient is in the vicinity. What if she lives in another country? What if your gift is an advertisement for yourself? What if, not knowing what you want—besides an ice-cube machine—you are incapable of imagining what she wants, and end up insulting her by choosing the plastic, the campy or the obscene?

Moreover, you have learned from your friends that among them are artists in gift-giving, haunters of shops, mood-detectives who have lavished such stamina and enterprise on a present for you that their love astounds. You expect to open up a secret of your character; inside, instead, you discover grace. Surprise! Not an ambush, but a valentine or a credit card. And so you take your daughter aside. She probably wants a chemistry set or bionic kneecaps. You are a mendicant, asking for alms of another order:

"What do I want for Christmas? I want you to listen to Beethoven's last quartets instead of the Grateful Dead. I want Bobby Kennedy to be alive. I want to be Russell Baker or Leo Tolstoy, whichever comes first. I want to go to Mars. I want to be your father."

Cheevered

Call him Dmitri. We have to call him something, and he has never been satisfied with his real name, which is, like Bill or Pete or Tom, a thin name, almost a pronoun, all edge, lacking a dimension, no muscle, no hair, no fat pads. Dmitri he associates with the calisthenics of the soul in nineteenth-century Russian novels.

Anyway, Dmitri had to go to Chicago. On the whole, he preferred never leaving New York. And if he had to leave New York, he wanted to go to some other imperial city, Paris or Rome or Baghdad, where the citizens knew that they were at the center of things. But it is sometimes necessary—no one had ever explained why—to go to Chicago, which teems with people wearing plastic identification badges pinned to their lapels to remind themselves of who they are supposed to be.

Having concluded his business in Chicago, Dmitri presented himself early at O'Hare Airport for what he thought of as re-entry. Would New York this time have discovered in his absence that it could get along without him? There was time to buy a book, a sort of print pill one takes to dissolve the sense of dislocation. And so he made his mistake. It is easy to say in retrospect that he should have purchased a copy of *The Hite Report* and found out how American women really feel about sex.

But Dmitri wasn't sure he really wanted to know how American women really felt about sex; it seemed an invasion of their privacy. Besides, the mystery of Woman was one of the few things he worshipped, along with the energy of New York and the prose of John Cheever. Instead of *The Hite Report,* he bought a paperback collection of John Cheever short stories called *The Brigadier and the Golf Widow.* Thus equipped, he was ready to be airborne, the mind a particle on the jet stream, the body strapped down for the inevitable steamed steak and the consolations of alcohol.

There was a delay on the ground. Why is there always a delay in Chicago, and never a delay in Paris? Dmitri read. By mere chance—and there is nothing more terrible in this world than mere chance—what Dmitri read was a story of a man whose gift, or trick, for getting along in life inexplicably deserts him. Now, this is characteristic Cheever: dark currents in the swimming pool, skeletons in the liquor closet, domesticated desperation, plaintive Sisypheans on a plastic slope, losing their grip when luck, or charm, runs out.

But Dmitri was disquieted. The man in the story hadn't a clue as to why the world suddenly mistrusted or actively disdained him; why, for instance, on going to a cocktail party in the luxury apartment house of friends, he was directed by the doorman to the service entrance. How had he managed before? He couldn't remember, although he was trying to even as he returned at night to his suburban estate and his own dogs devoured him.

Luck, charm, chance, dividends from trust funds, accidents of birth, the roll of the dice of the genes, fingernails of DNA, credit cards of a blameless personality—all canceled. Your license is revoked. You have been found out. According to the C.I.A. or Ralph Nader or Sigmund Freud or Hua Kuo-feng or *The Hite Report* or God, you are now and always have been unserious and insincere. At last in the sky, and rather shaky, Dmitri asked the stewardess for two of those little toy bottles of Scotch.

The stewardess hated him.

Why? He hadn't asked for extra ice. He'd said please. Courtesy was his coin, and inoffensiveness his style. But she hated him, and he knew it. In the lamp of her loathing, he was paralyzed, like a rabbit on the road at night in the lights of a truck. He tried, and failed, to hate her back. (He admired stewardesses; they are competent.) You are constructed of nylon and plywood, he thought. But she wasn't. Except in her dealings with him—a Scotch bottle snatched away before it had been entirely emptied, the steamed steak upside down—she was the personification of perkiness, Mary Tyler Moore on roller skates.

Good Lord, it had happened. Cheevered, just like that, as though his life were an anecdote to which he had forgotten the punch line, and they sneered. The approval of strangers was crucial to Dmitri; he survived because of it. Which is why he made sure to have exact change for buses, was a conscientious over-tipper in taxicabs and restaurants, talked to women at dinner parties about their children, knew how to be sad when it counted, showered once a day, remembered to say I love you.

He should have known he had been Cheevered when the last ten twin-packs of seven-and-a-half-ounce Wise potato chips turned out not to be as crisp as he preferred. He had imagined a breakdown in quality control at Berwick, Pennsylvania. Instead, they were out to get him. And if airline stewardesses and Wise potato chips were out to get him, what about New York? He would, he knew, come back to a block on which every garbage can but his own had been emptied by sanitation workers with Mafia connections; to a Chinese laundry that had been taken over by Albanians or Arabs; to a zip code that added up to an audit of his psychic tax returns; to children who had figured out that he was a coward; to a wife who was reading *The Hite Report*. Devastated, he punched the button for the stewardess.

"You are hostile," said Dmitri. "Yes," said Samantha. "How have I offended you?" said Dmitri. "You boarded," said Samantha, "with a youth-fare ticket, and then you ordered Scotch, and I don't like people who cheat." "Wrong," said Dmitri; "I haven't been that young for sixteen years, and you can check it out."

Samantha checked it out. She had mistaken his identity. So, perhaps, had he. She fetched him a third Scotch, on the wings of whatever. And then he was home, and young again.

Good News

Let's say that Dmitri is a friend of the novelist Reynolds Price. For Christmas, 1976, Reynolds Price has given his friends a handsomely printed, privately published little book called *The Good News According to Mark*. It is a new translation by Mr. Price, from the ancient Greek manuscripts, of the Gospel According to St. Mark. It could not have come to Dmitri's house at a better time.

Dmitri's fourteen-year-old son has just proclaimed his atheism. The principles of logic are to Dmitri's son what the music of Bach is to Dmitri—beautiful, self-justifying, the architecture of the universe—and he has decided not to buy the idea of a supernatural first cause or prime mover. Life, he thinks, probably got started when a lightning bolt or a blast of cosmic radiation roiled the waters of the primordial earth soup and molecules found out they could replicate themselves.

Ordinarily, Dmitri takes almost as much pleasure in the workings of his son's mind as his son does: the gritty premise, the brave syllogism, snap, crackle and pop, absolute truth for breakfast. And the logic is familiar. That same logic led Dmitri, when he was sixteen, to a spiritual impasse, from which he sought to extricate himself by delivering the sermon on Youth Sunday at St. Thomas of Canterbury Episcopal Church. A congregation of the flabby and the stupefied heard Dmitri through his acne babble on of Kierkegaard and *Either/Or*, of leaps of faith, as though souls were broad jumpers. Members of the congregation actually grinned. Not even the vicar, who afterward patted him on the head, had realized the sermon was a cry for help. To what had Dmitri leaped? Bingo?

And so he went off to college, where they taught the Bible as literature, and *Either/Or* was a false dichotomy, and faith was in bad taste. It seems to be the purpose of college to acquaint us with the abyss as an aesthetic, not a moral, category; to domesticate the mysteries; to propose, in the words of Céline, that "There is nothing, Monsieur Baryton, between the penis and mathematics, nothing at all!" Dmitri took courses in irony.

Dmitri's son has grown up in a secular household. A church to him is the place he went for a memorial service for his great-grandfather, which is also the closest he has come to the experience of death. At least it was a New England church, and not one of the modern ones that look like drive-in restaurants. His ethics are standardized. Basically, his father is asking him to behave as George Orwell would have in a similar situation. He is thoroughly decent. He just hasn't been introduced to the concept of Original Sin, that "black conceit" without which, according to Melville, "no man can weigh this world" and "strike the uneven balance."

But he hasn't had much to weigh, has he? Wearing his atheism like a campaign button or a boutonnière, as though he were on his way to a rally for mental hygiene, he is a stranger to evil, tragedy and senselessness. He has been disappointed, yes, and hurt, yes, and bewildered, certainly, and on those occasions either his father or his mother has explained: "As John F. Kennedy once said, life is unfair." What a consolation! He hasn't yet confronted the irrational that, with a bloody claw, scatters all axioms.

Which is why Dmitri, at the breakfast table, gnaws a crust of qualm. It is not simply that Christmas stares him in the eye, and that Frosty and Rudolph and Bloomingdale's and the Grinch have stolen his Christmas from him. Nor is it merely that his son, his excuse for being, innocent of birth and death and discrepancy and of everything but yesterday, pronounces so confidently on ultimate matters. (Do we no longer have to go to college to unlearn metaphysics? Are we instant Sartres, Reddi-Wipped in the womb, authentic in Pampers, anti-heroes prior to nursery school, alone before we've met anybody?)

Nor is it even that good friends have recently suffered a death, an unfairness so stupid and irreversible that Dmitri can't explain it to himself, much less to his son. (In forgetting how to worship, have we forgotten how to grieve? Is throwing a tantrum better than lighting a candle?)

No. He has neglected to talk to his son of final things. They talk of haircuts, homework, TV programs, sports scores, eating habits. Dmitri hasn't dared admit that the standardized ethics of his household have a history; that the cross in his imagination might be a growing tree; that sacrifice and reciprocity, grace and mercy, love and justice, are more than just ideas or deductions or theories waiting around for proofs. They are dreams that have survived our knowledge of ourselves. They are scales on which we measure our worth. They have even outlasted a church of inquisitors and clerks.

If Dmitri knew how, he would say to his son that, granted, religion is wishful thinking, but there is no other kind of thinking, and it seeks ceremony. Just as there are tools that we trust, that are true, so there are symbols that are sacred, in which our hopes repose, true, too, and enduring. Look, he would say, at the shadow in European painting, or at cathedral light. Listen to Bach, or to Handel's *Messiah*. They aren't arguments, any more than the imagination of the Tao is an argument. They do, though, bear witness to an unarguable need, a passion. We wonder.

How does one begin such a conversation with one's son? *The Good News According to Mark* is a start. The Mark of Reynolds Price is more colloquial, and the Jesus earthier, than King James would have them. To one's son one says: "Do you remember the parable about not putting new wine into old bottles? The bottles would burst? It doesn't make sense, does it? But according to Reynolds Price, what Mark really says that Jesus said is 'skins,' not 'bottles.' In those days, they drank wine out of skins, which dried up and cracked. You have to go back to the original Greek. But Mark was there. He was a kind of secretary and interpreter for Peter. Peter was a *witness*, and maybe Mark was, too."

And one's son, a cat among proofs, knows suddenly that there *is* a document, evidence, and that, as Mr. Price puts it, "a great *thing* happened in the presence of human witnesses who, however slow to comprehend, eventually did so and survived to tell the tale." And one's son wonders, too.

Plastic

When Dmitri went berserk, his family, familiar with his frenzies, knew exactly what to do. They lowered him from the rafters, laid him out on the rug, folded him up in sections like an American flag, and gave him a washrag soaked in sour mash to chew on. While hot and cold running daughters sang madrigals and quoted Pasternak, Dmitri was heard through the washrag to shout: *"Écrasez l'infâme!"*

He had been trying to get the pinball machine to work. It was one of those plastic contraptions, made in Quemoy or Matsu by imperialist lackeys, smuggled by atomic submarine to the home of the brave and disguised as a Christmas present which, on the unwrapping, inscrutably malfunctions. Battery transplants hadn't helped. Nor had stomping on it. His jumping up and down on the pinball machine, in fact, had caused Dmitri to ravel himself in the macramé plant-hanger, where but for the intervention of his family he would have strangled.

By nightfall they judged him calm enough to remove the wash-rag and put him on a bottle. "Listen," he said, and the light in his eyes was that of a radio dial looking for a clear signal: "Plastic is not sincere. Plastic has no memory. The wheel remembers the water, and the mill remembers the wind, and the glass remembers the sand, and the beer remembers the barley. But what does plastic remember? The urea from which it derives? Thin chance!"

"The credit card remembers everything," said one of his daughters.

"Shut up," said Dmitri. "The credit card stole all the sex from money. What was once a metaphor for labor is now merely a movement of information: tittle-tattle." He pointed to their Christmas tree: "You made birds and stars out of paper and wood, and globes out of eggshells, a cincture of cranberry and a torque of corn. The tree drinks and the fir breathes and the totem recapitulates phylogeny—which is a hell of a lot more than can be said for that pinball machine."

On the whole, his children would have preferred a rerun of *The Brady Bunch*, but fathers needed an inordinate amount of forbearance.

"It's my fault," said Dmitri with the usual arrogance, the greedy guilt, of fathers. "You are not to blame for having been packaged, as infants, in nonwoven cellulose disposable diapers and boilable vinyl-lined waterproof acetate pants. Nor the Dacron polyester shift of your mother and the prefab Melamite laminate countertop of our kitchen, all over which you burped; the bathinette, like Tupperware, into which we plopped you like leftovers; the Thermoglas container that turned your milk blue and the synthetic nipple by which you were pacified.

"I heard you cry, at the eye of the Nite-Lite Bakelite illuminated wall switch in your nursery, from your Sterofoam polyurethane bed pad, beneath the fine-mesh elasticized white nylon mosquito netting, inside your Orlon acrylic sleeper with the skid-resistant plastic soles on your little bootee feet. I ought to have known that your cry was a question. Orlon acrylic! Dacron polyester! Arnel triacetate! Rayon! Neoprene! Vibron! Vyrene! Santeen and Spandex! *Why*, you wanted to know, vat-dyed, nonskid, two-plied, rib-knit, snap-shouldered, sanitized, mercerized, Sanforized, shrink-resistant and machine-washable, *why am I the only thing in the world that smells?*

"No wonder, then, that when you were old enough to creep, you did so in the direction of the bathroom, from which, out of the polyethylene diaper pail, you stole the cake deodorant and took it back to your crib to sleep with." Dmitri's sob was dyspeptic. "To smell," he said, "to remember, to be sincere or edible, to grow or experience motion, to have grain or be tickled, to reflect or sustain rainbows—is life! Organic life! Do not, I beg you, dwell in the blue rooms of the Winter Palace of plastic, among pinball machines, eating electric light and passing it through your bladder, excreting it into vats from which new compounds of plastic will be synthesized, gadgets beyond good and evil."

His daughters promised they wouldn't, and hugged his feet,

but he kicked them aside on his way to the telephone, which he yanked out by its jack and cast into the fireplace. "Change, and transformation," he explained. The telephone was followed by a wastepaper basket, a comb, some cups and a picnic hamper, a cushion covered in Naugahyde, the seat from a toilet, containers of ketchup and detergent, trivets, a tablecloth and a toothbrush. "Observe," he said. For kindling, he added pine cones and the latest, the last, edition of Dorothy Schiff. Then he ignited.

"You will notice that plastic is dishonest. It doesn't burn. It does not transform or transcend itself. It blackens and cracks. It is deathless, never having been alive. Without memory, it is immobile and immutable, the smug stuff of the laboratory, like a French novel. It can't cry. Even now, it is poisoning the dolphins. When the Martians land, and analyze our garbage, they will imagine us to have been without seed or season. If, with my hands and my feet, I try to break the pinball machine, it splinters. I would rather die with a silver bullet, than with a plastic sliver in my heart."

Dmitri clearly felt bad. He gripped himself by his elbows, as if to forestall unhinging. "The floors of the Winter Palace," he said, "are paved with linoleum. The walls are petrified lymph. Plastic, like cancer, conspires at a metastatic shift. My dreams are to be shut up inside a see-through coffin, stoppered, Baggied. It may already be too late. For this brave new year, I wish you blood on your linoleum, pigment and ligature, passion and music, fire and sand, seeds and seasons, asparagus and snow, rope and orange juice. I wish you tools instead of toys, and honor, and thumbprints."

"Organic father," said his children, "you must be hungry." They brought him a Spam sandwich on Less Bread, with a side of Pringles and a Diet Pepsi.

Bowling

Dmitri went bowling. You laugh? Zipper your lip. Not all of us, when we want to do something with our children, can afford to sail off like William F. Buckley, Jr.—see his new book, *Airborne* —on a *Cyrano* or a *Suzy Wong* or a *Panic*, with nothing to worry about but the electric bilge pump and the battered gooseneck and the astigmatizer on our sextant, while reading *Moby Dick*. Some of us must be less thrilling.

There are those afternoons, those weekends, when the bottom falls out of the lives of our children. We look around, and see them standing in holes of sadness. Too old for *Sesame Street* and too young for sex, they tend to depend on friends. As Dmitri's daughter has explained, "One friend is all you need. But without that one, life is hell." And friends betray. They go to the country, or the birthday parties of enemies, or reject you for two weeks.

Nor can "organized activities" plug these holes of sadness. The activities of middle-class children in this city have been organized already to the point of zombiism. With their lessons in dance, tennis, piano, carpentry and horseback riding, their pottery classes and French-speaking day camps, their summer school courses in film history and remedial etiquette, our children are drudges of self-improvement. It is as if their leisure were a beast to be tamed, saddled, leashed. We groom them like dogs for a show, and ought to be ashamed of ourselves.

On a recent friendless afternoon, the children had consumed all the junk food in the house. They had tired of reading Tolkien and Tacitus and Wonder Woman comic books. They had broken the yogurt-maker and clogged the peanut butter machine and gummed up the TV attachment that lets you play Ping-Pong or take target practice on the blank screen. (We fill their space with electric toys so that, exhausted by their self-improvement, they won't have to move around much.) So they petitioned their father for a cure for sadness and ennui.

Bowling

It was chancy. Are fathers, with their cuffs and kisses, friends? Like most American fathers, Dmitri either pretended to be too busy to spend much time with his children or he went on binges, machine-gun bursts of love that mowed down their guarded expectations. They didn't realize that in his awkwardness he was afraid he might hurt them. He didn't realize that they forgave him his awkwardness in advance. What else had they ever known?

As it happens, Dmitri had just decided it was time for him to be more than a friendly cloud floating over the landscape of their childhood. He wanted to be some weather, a wind, some water, a rock. Surveying the possibilities, he disdained Monopoly (hateful), rowing in Central Park (too cold), blackjack (tedious unless real money was involved) and movies (Mel Brooks caused tumors).

"Let's," said Dmitri, "go bowling."

They had never heard of bowling. He himself hadn't bowled since he was a young pimple maturing in Long Beach, California. Ah, youth! On the beach, among surfers and sun bunnies and Cub Scouts threatening one another's throats with corkscrews, he had felt inadequate. Bad at volleyball, what choice had he other than to bowl? Striking out, pasty-faced, in purple stretch pants and bone-colored suède leather shoes and a black shantung jacket with eagles and serpents all over it, he had acquired a male role. Briefly, he had been a punk.

Which he neglected to tell the children. He explained instead the rules of bowling. He was historical, letting them in on the Polynesian ritual of Ula Maika; and sociological, going on about the female factory workers who discovered the game in World War II while the men were overseas; and philosophical, babbling of *nostalgie de la boue* and the Pythagorean pyramids into which the pins are clustered; and technocratic, on the replacing of teen-aged pinboys by Brunswick automatic pinsetters: and philologic, on the substitution of "lane" for "alley" so that families would consider a trip there to be respectable.

Like most American fathers, Dmitri explained too much. Like most American children, his kids didn't want to do anything or eat anything they hadn't done or gorged before. But they knew him to be in the grip of one of his preposterous enthusiasms. They went along to make sure he was safe on the streets.

Dmitri's enthusiasms are often more than the world is prepared to tolerate, and the world has a way of cutting him down to size. He was not surprised at having to rent special bowling shoes. But to be compelled to surrender one of his street shoes, as a kind of collateral, before they would give him the bowling shoes, was an insult. Did people steal bowling shoes, even in New York? And to be obliged to hobble, one shoe on and one shoe missing, from the vacant-faced poonghie at the check-in desk to his assigned "lane," in front of his children, with a hole in his naked sock, offended him in his dignity.

His children didn't notice. They didn't notice because they had realized that they were actually going to enjoy themselves. Imagine being liberated into a huge room where for a couple of hours the object is to knock something down, and loud noises are not only inevitable but desirable, and there is always someone nearby more incompetent than you are. "Dad, this was a great idea," said his son, to whom great ideas were usually hamburgers. The din was theirs to swim in; they made waves with their glee.

Dmitri watched them with tears in his eyes and holes in his socks. If not great, it was at least a good idea, and it had been Dmitri's. Once upon a time, he thought, I was a punk, and now I am a father. If I am not, in the lives of my children, the weather, water, wind or rock, perhaps I am the Brunswick automatic pinsetter who picks them up after they've been knocked down. He felt better about himself, and if doing something with his children made him feel better about himself, he would have to try it more often.

The Imperial City

My daughter, for reasons that are nobody's business but my own, spends much of her time in Florida, which I imagine through a mythic mist to consist of hotels, marching bands, alligators and Cuban exiles with C.I.A. connections, under a boring sun. Who knows? I was in Boca Raton once, where it rained four days on the just and the unjust, the polo ponies and the putting green. We sat around listening to our brains rot.

Anyway, she was off the other night to the airport and her peninsula, bundled up like a Russian, commuting as it were between the capital of work and the World of Disney. In her suitcase was a T-shirt stenciled "I Love New York." This surprised. It surprised because, like her brother, she has always considered this city a sort of penal colony to which she had been unfairly sentenced for the winter months of her childhood—dirt in the air and dung in the streets and riots in the schools—whereas the real criminal was her father, who couldn't seem to find a job anyplace where there were strawberries and rabbits.

How did one explain to one's daughter that one valued New York precisely because it wasn't cute?

Now she has changed her mind, along with her address. It would be nice to think that she has changed her mind because of the Christmas tree in Rockefeller Center, or the New York City Ballet to which she is partial, or the Guinness museum in the Empire State Building, or Zero Mostel, or me. But no. She has changed her mind because of delicatessens, movie houses, bookstores, hot pretzels and the crosstown bus. She had been, without knowing it, a citizen of an imperial city, capable on whim of donning her down jacket, like a pair of wings, and flapping off on errands of mercy or revenge or jelly beans. In the imperial city, she was a little adult. Until she went away, she had no idea how difficult it is for a child to be an adult in the great American outback of automobiles and expressways, of shopping centers as remote as Mars.

One forgets that our children learn to "read" the city almost as soon as they master their primers. The streets are a lesson in simple addition and subtraction. The bus routes and the subway system are no more complicated than a TV schedule. This kind of reading, like any other kind, liberates. To be liberated into New York, where anything that exists can somehow be got at, is just as exhilarating as to be liberated into literature, to be handed a key to all those boxes of trapped words. My children these days return to New York with lists of things they want—sesame-seed bagels, clarinet reeds, biographies of Cromwell—and find they can secure them without waiting for the big people to mount a car caravan as elaborate in the preparation as Kitchener's advance on Khartoum. New York, says my son, is a city where you don't have to *subscribe* to magazines.

Why is it, on returning in a cab from the airport after putting one's daughter on a plane to Gainesville, one wants to apologize to the driver and to God and to Kant's categorical imperative?

I should have been thinking about an article some magazine had asked me to write: "Remarriage—Is It Good for Israel?" Instead, I was remembering a conversation among seven-year-old girls at the breakfast table, the morning after a birthday-party sleepover. I had stopped on the stairs to eavesdrop. They compared notes on houses, rented apartments, condominiums and cooperatives. They compared notes on yogurt. And they compared notes on fathers. Of the six girls, only one had a "live-in father." Those girls are ten years old now. My daughter knew exactly where to find them. On Tuesdays and Thursdays, when their school recesses for lunch, they go to Jackson Hole or the Spaghetti Works. The other days of the week they rotate in one another's homes. They are New York children, competent and wary.

Back in my city, Monday night, I watched public television, perhaps because, the last I heard, it wasn't yet owned by Rupert Murdoch or the Saudi Arabians. There on the screen was Tom Wolfe's idiosyncratic and entertaining visual essay on the Los Angeles inside his head. Having grown up around L.A., I was mesmerized. Wolfe caught the anarchy, which is to Los Angeles what smugness used to be for San Francisco. Los Angeles, Boston, Chicago, San Francisco, Washington, D.C.—it took me three-quarters of my life to get to New York. From the cities we've left behind, like the clothes we would no longer be caught dead in and the garbage we put out on the streets, someone is building a dossier, writing an indictment. We will be found out.

The thought occurred: My daughter knows as little of Los Angeles as I know of Gainesville, Florida. For her, it's an airport. Not so, my son. Several years ago he went there with me for some symposium on Mary Tyler Moore. A friend, twenty years old and recently divorced, met us at the airport. Her ex-husband, she said, had taken up with a seventeen-year-old, given her birth-control pills in an Excedrin bottle, which her father had opened when he had a headache. The father felt odd, assumed hallucinogens and called the police.

We visited another friend, a U.C.L.A. professor who had just left his wife and child, was about to fly to England and had had his stash of marijuana baked into a batch of oatmeal cookies by his girlfriend, to get through customs. We were returned to the airport by my brother, who has since tilted at his own satanic mills. As a going-away present, my brother gave me an LSD capsule, which I flushed down a toilet on the plane over the Grand Canyon. Or was it a Lascaux cave? When my son was asked in New York what he thought of Los Angeles, he said: "Birth-control pills in the Excedrin bottle and marijuana in the oatmeal cookies. Really weird."

Really, weirdness runs me through, like a spear. I examine my lapels. I wonder if, like sesame-seed bagels, I am on my daughter's list of things to get in New York. We are a city of eight million people, and that, I am sorry to say, is two too few.

New York Women

We gave a dinner party. It was for a distinguished artist in his middle years, a refugee from marital wars, suddenly displaced and wanting companionship. The idea of the dinner party was to introduce him to several intelligent and charming women who happened at the moment to be unattached. It was probably a stupid idea, but most of my friends in this city are intelligent and charming women who happen at the moment to be unattached, and I can only marry one at a time.

Why these women are unattached doesn't matter. Perhaps their husbands came home from the office one day with a mid-life crisis, like a BankAmericard. Perhaps, instead, the women one night decided that the self-pity of their husbands was a tyrannical bore. Perhaps, even now, a psychiatrist somewhere is sitting down to dip his pen in their wounds and write a best-seller about the ecstasies of self. It doesn't matter. We are all amateurs at marriage the first time around; some of us are just luckier amateurs than others.

My friends have hermeneutic and erotic depths. They are adults. That is, they are old enough to have voted for John F. Kennedy, and when they talk to you they do not bat their eyelashes, and when they chew their food, they keep their mouths closed, and they can be counted on to have read some books that weren't written by Carlos Castaneda. Although they wear a motley of temperaments—whimsical, ironic, gabby, brave—none on leaving college dropped her brain in a sugar canister to see if it would ferment. They went to work in law and science and teaching and journalism. There are calluses on their experience, which improves the grip. They know how to hold on to you when you are falling apart, if you are worth the effort.

Many have children. When they come to the house, they stop at the telephone and remove an earring before cradling the receiver between their shoulder and chin. They are calling to say good night to their children. I suppose that, with pierced ears, this gesture of removing an earring to place a call will disappear; technology is the enemy of grace. I also suppose that earrings themselves will come to be judged as subversive of radical sisterhood. So perhaps will children be deemed an impediment to the brave new narcissism. It seems to me that people who run around saying they don't want children advertise an unearned smugness, a lack of imagination, but I am often wrong.

These female adults, then, had been gathered for the distinguished artist. They were waiting for him with their opinions on culture and politics. Like W.C. Fields, he would have to fight his way through "a wall of human flesh, dragging my goat and my canoe behind me," even to get to the cheese dip. Unexpectedly and alas, the distinguished artist arrived with a sex kitten on his elbow. This sex kitten, at least twenty-five years his junior, had no opinions, but she spent the entire evening adhered to him on the couch, nibbling his unpierced ear instead of the cheese dip. He left early, on a gust of passion.

Only the week before, he had wanted companionship. Is there a tribal drum among the young, announcing the availability of men? In the night, a tom-toming: Distinguished artist on Upper West Side has been alone for two hours! At dawn, in front of his apartment building, are busloads of Bennington nymphets, all majoring in Stevie Wonder and the new morality. He won't make it to the subway station.

All right, men in this city can't stand loneliness, even for a week. They hang around like Venetian blinds, waiting for someone to pull their string. After the first carton of takeout Chinese food or bowl of frozen chili on a Friday night, they start baying at the television set. If they actually remember how, after years of hiding behind their mothers and their secretaries, they may even bring themselves to stab their fingers into those little holes in the face of the telephone and dial for help. But must help always arrive in the form of a sex kitten, a Tinkertoy, a disposable "relationship" with a slab of marzipan their daughter's age, her head full of magazine articles and movie stills? Why don't they take as much time solving the problem of their loneliness as they spend studying a menu in a restaurant?

What, I am asking, will happen to my friends, the grownups? They sit in my living room, histories of triumph and disaster, anthologies of wit and forbearance. They have been some places and heard some music. They are wise and kind and competent and *complicated*—and lonely, too. If they weren't in my living room, they would be in somebody else's, making the world briefly a better place, or home writing a novel, or at the theater, or visiting a gallery, or drinking white wine at a reception for a Moog Synthesizer that sounds like a hyena in heat. They subsidize, in fact, our culture with the space in their lives, their attentiveness, the grain of their character.

The last thing they need is little boys, and the men in this city tend to be little boys, with wooden swords. What will happen to my friends, I fear, is that they will settle for affairs with men who seem, for a while anyway, almost as grown-up as my friends; men who seem not to be afraid of women who can remember Adlai Stevenson; men not unacquainted with irony and gratitude and solace. These men will, of course, be married to someone else. If my friends are lucky—if, that is, they don't spend the rest of their lives in hotel rooms on spurious business trips, or alone on Club Med vacations during the family holiday seasons—they will have helped to cause the next generation of intelligent and charming women who happen at the moment to be unattached.

Everybody deserves better than this. It takes a long time and a lot of practice to become a human being. It is outrageous that, having finally done so, you discover that no other human being seems to need you.

About Cats (I)

It is Egypt. I am surrounded by cats. They tick like clocks, like bombs. Actually, it is not Egypt. It is the kitchen, at seven in the morning. I am boiling the coffee in order to feel bad because we are supposed to be boycotting coffee. We boycott South African diamonds instead. The Siamese whines. She is on top of the broom closet. The other, problematical cat, the long-haired black one who recently amazed herself with a litter of kittens, crouches in the middle of the round table, pretending to be profound. Anything that eats flies cannot be profound. The black cat, the wineglass and the pepper mill make the table look like a bad Impressionist painting. I sent a memo to God pointing out that kitchen tables should not look like bad Impressionist paintings, at least before breakfast. God did not reply.

According to G. C. Lichtenberg (1799), "What astonished him was that cats should have two holes cut in their coats exactly at the place where their eyes were."

The rest of the house snores. I hope this includes the kittens, but probably not. At six weeks, they know how to pull themselves up the carpet on the stairs, and could be anywhere. They tire easily, however, and instead of hiding to sleep it off, they just drop in their tracks. Be careful where you put your foot. What seems a sock might be a grenade. It is snowing again. I cannot find it in my heart to feel sorry for Buffalo. Buffalo has never felt sorry for me. Let it blizzard. Secretly, I enjoy the whine of tires, like Siamese, trapped in city snowbanks, the spinning of wheels on ice. Alternate-side-of-the-street frustration makes my day. These people—inside their tin symbolic phalluses; narrowing our lives with their double parking, their grease spoor and their cologne of carburetor; blowing their horns like their noses or their minds, as though they were mastodons with sinus headaches—these people are being punished. Like Evel Knievel. The sports page says that Evel Knievel broke his collarbone. I can find it in my heart to feel sorry for the thirteen sharks. At seven in the morning, I am not bittersweet.

Yesterday, across the crowded lobby of the New York Times Building, my friend Seymour Hersh shouted at me: "Listen, Dmitri, did it ever occur to you that I've got troubles, too?" Very funny. Tell it to Sidney Horshak. I want to explain to Hersh how hard it is to be bittersweet once a week. Our wounds are greedy mouths; they would devour us, like the cats.

The cats want to be fed. Since the arrival of the kittens, the responsibility for feeding the cats has gone to the ten-year-old in our house. This is because she wants the cats, all five of them, to stay in her room at night, and they will only do so if the food, water and kitty litter are in that room as well. The ten-year-old, fortunately, sleeps as though someone had hit her on the head with a croquet mallet.

Now, the cats know perfectly well that I no longer feed them in the morning. Nevertheless, they mewl, and rub, and pace, and pounce. They even try to trip me. Their own convenience is the only compass they have ever bothered to consult. If they were radios, I would turn them off. Do they, like Evel Knievel, have collarbones? Of course not. Otherwise they wouldn't be able to hide behind the washing machine or inside a tennis sneaker whenever the doorbell rings.

That cats couldn't possibly have collarbones, shoulder blades, has probably been obvious to everybody else for years. I am lousy on the obvious. (In her fine novel *Speedboat*, Renata Adler asks: "What is the point? . . . The point has never quite been entrusted to me." Exactly. Being bittersweet means always having to say you're sorry.) Also, I never thought much about cats, nor they about me. From pets I want uncritical affection. That means a dog. And dogs don't belong in this city, not only because they pollute it, like cars, but because dogs deserve better than fire hydrants and steam heat. Dogs deserve trees and porcupines and vegetable rot and all those other things that make the countryside so boring. If I can't have a dog, I will settle for a television set.

What's the point of a pet who thinks he's better than you are?

About Cats (I)

Don't you get enough of that at the office? You will reply: Beauty. I watch the Siamese, in her imperial arrogance, lick her coat. A cat, then, is an *objet d'art*, a luxury item. Cats are certainly a leisure class. The French, Russian and Chinese revolutions were in vain, so far as cats are concerned. Every single one of them is a Sun King, a Pharaoh. They lack humility.

But cats came with the marital package. They climb on my suits. They sleep on my typewriter. If no one answers the telephone, they knock the receiver off the hook to make the ringing stop. And now there are kittens. Suddenly older than Egypt, the mother cat copes. It seems that half the world—little girls, old men, Jehovah's Witnesses—has come into the house to see the kittens. Kittens make people feel better. With all those tears of joy, we haven't had to water the plants in a month.

The coffee is fit for a Turk. I bring a mug of it to my beloved, for whom the dawn's early light is a personal affront, an insult. The kittens have gotten there first. They are playing king-of-the-mountain on a pillow. Each presides for a moment, then rolls off in the face of mock attack. Gulliver, who will belong to my daughter, hops up on the windowsill. (The others have been spoken for by friends, not including Seymour Hersh.) Gulliver regards the snow, and tries to wash a paw. His balance is imperfect. He tumbles from the sill, and somersaults. Eat your heart out, Walt Disney.

It occurs to me that if the mere fact of kittens makes us feel better, maybe we are better than we usually feel we are. If there is a chord in us that kittens strike, maybe there's one for justice, and for mercy, for sacrifice and reciprocity, kindness and respect. We may be full of music and too busy to listen to ourselves.

My beloved speaks: "My God, you've got that bittersweet look on your face again, and I haven't even brushed my teeth."

Oliver

And now for something completely different. Once upon a time I
was a technical public relations man. This means I wrote articles
about the products of my clients and placed those articles in trade
magazines. Trade magazines couldn't survive without free articles,
and a technical public relations man couldn't survive without a
book of clippings—cheap publicity—to show his client, and we
were all as solvent as we were unnecessary.

One of my clients in those days made an "elastomeric seat
suspension unit," really just a web of rubber strips you staple on a
furniture frame to save yourself the cost of springs or cushions. I
went South, where most of the furniture factories live, to write
articles and take pictures of our product in action. I won't tell you
what happened in Mount Airy or in Myrtle Beach, but somewhere
in the vicinity of Winston-Salem I had a revelation.

It happened at a factory specializing in brand-new antique
furniture. How does one "antique" a brand-new table or chair?
We went down in an elevator to a windowless room. There was a
huge black man in boxer shorts. He had a three-foot length of
chain, studded with nails. He was given a table, and he whipped
it with his chain. The pockmarks were guaranteed random. Stain
or lacquer was then applied. The table-whipper enjoyed his job,
I was told over mint juleps at the country club by my hosts, who
were nice people for racists.

This was before Jimmy Carter. All right?

If you were downtown on East Twenty-second Street the
other Saturday morning, you might have seen us in our adversity,
under clumps of winter clothes, our faces lit with white fire like
the martyrs of logic in a Wallace Stevens poem, kicking at the
barred door of Draftsman Furniture, Inc. We weren't waiting for
Lefty or Godot. We were waiting for Oliver.

I've never met Oliver, although the woman in my life assures me he exists. Nor have I achieved Oliver on the telephone, although I've tried dozens of times. When someone actually bestirs himself to answer the phone at the Draftsman, after as many as forty rings, that someone seems to be Richie, who can't check your invoice because the invoices are locked up in Oliver's office, and Oliver has the only key, and, like Macavity the Mystery Cat, *Oliver's not there!* To believe that Oliver will return your calls is to believe in the Great Pumpkin, the Tooth Fairy, the orgone box and the Piltdown man.

There is a hole in my living room, a space of longing. In the night I feel it throb, the way an old wound remembers a lost love or an amputated limb, and sometimes I hear it cry. "Couch," it says at two in the morning, "couch." I call this hole Oliver.

Yes, I know. In the current issue of *Esquire*, a friend asks Nora Ephron, "Does everyone who gets married talk about furniture?" Ephron replies: "No. Only for a while. After that you talk about pistachio nuts." And here I am talking about furniture, and you would probably prefer a column on pistachio nuts. But in the evening, after the children have been perfused, when I would like to sit by the fire and drink Irish coffee and listen to Mozart and read Wallace Stevens, pistachio nuts seem in the larger scheme of things to be so much lint in God's bellybutton, whereas a couch is a canoe.

This much is certain in a problematic world: on August 3, 1976, we bought a couch at Draftsman Furniture, Inc., 12 East Twenty-second Street, I am staring at the canceled check. Delivery, from the South, was promised for September 25th. But we are New Yorkers, crystallized cynics: with a promise and some Kleenex, you can blow your nose. We knew it wouldn't arrive September 25th, and it didn't. We set the alarm clocks of our anxiety for mid-October. Even Macy's doesn't take that long.

They were still answering the telephone at the Draftsman on the ides of October, but couldn't help us. Only Oliver could help us, and *Oliver's not there!* Nor was he for the next twenty-seven phone calls until one memorable Sunday morning when he must have picked up the phone by mistake, hoping for his mother. Oliver assured the woman in my life that he would investigate the whereabouts of our couch. Unfortunately, the factory down South wasn't open on Sunday. He would get back to us.

That there was an Oliver was nice to know. We never heard from him again. A week later Richie told me that Oliver had married and was on his honeymoon, apparently having taken his invoices with him. I like marriages. I hope he has a couch. We wanted a couch to fill the hole in our living room when we were wed in early November. We wanted one for Thanksgiving, when rumor had it that Oliver was back in town. Presently, we will have wanted one for Christmas. Perhaps Easter? "Is the spot on the floor, there, wine or blood / And whichever it may be, is it mine?" asked Wallace Stevens. I hope he didn't ask Oliver.

Since Thanksgiving, they don't answer at the Draftsman. You get a busy signal, call back, and *Oliver's not there!* Which is why the other Saturday morning I went to East Twenty-second Street. Of course, the Draftsman was closed for alterations. Of course, the sidewalk swarmed with customers in an advanced stage of anxiety because their couches had been lost in orbit somewhere between Winston-Salem and Wallace Stevens. Rather more surprisingly, there were also woodworkers from Secaucus, New Jersey, with a truck that groaned of benches and six-piece living-room sets. The workers wanted to deliver and collect; the customers wanted to seize and abscond; Oliver—"Is my thought a memory, not alive?" (Wallace Stevens)—was tried in absentia. We couldn't break down the door.

Whether or not there really is an Oliver, I will find him. And when I do, having had my revelation in the windowless room so many years ago, I will "antique" him.

Youth

Youth dropped in on us the other night, after dinner. Youth had curly locks, and eyes that had seen the floors of some oceans, and he spoke the latest foreign language: Like, man, you know, laid back. In his steerhide motorcycle jacket with the snap-on lamb collar, his tie-dyed bell-bottom dungarees, his calfskin Wellington boots, Youth was so together that the rest of us felt left out.

We were fortunate. Had Youth come by the evening before, he would have caught us playing bridge. The only games one is permitted to play these days are backgammon and aikido. Bridge, in particular, suggests the bourgeois institution of marriage: couples filing two by two onto an Ark with a hole in its hull. If the hard rain of history is falling, Youth will climb into his guitar as though it were a kayak, and go where the water flows.

As it was, we were in the company of real people—a novelist, a newspaper reporter, a professor of child psychology, a producer of television documentaries. The conversation was a kind of whittling on our work, to see what shape it might assume, to follow the grain. If we were modest, it was not to the extent of despising ourselves. We felt, on the whole, that we had done more good than harm, at least recently.

Then why did Youth—who chose to sit on a stepladder against the wall, outside our murmuring circle; who gulped from a can of the Uncola as we clutched our brandy snifters; who was innocent of birth and death and Beethoven and Jackie Robinson; who hadn't failed because he hadn't tried, although he was forever promising to get around to it; who seemed to have been sculpted out of a block of vanilla ice cream, no knotholes; on whom advantages fell like leaves off our October—why did Youth make us feel guilty?

He wasn't telling. He just sat. What had he been up to? Well, he had been to California. He was always going to California or the movies. What had he found there? He had found a number of things that knocked him out. He was always being knocked out by things, whereas we had lived our lives trying to roll with the punch; we wobbled. What had knocked him out? Well, it was hard to put into words. Youth was "into actualizing myself." Western psychology and Eastern mysticism had to be reconciled.

Even to look him in the eye, we had to crane our necks, as if hoisting tons of scrap culture—Freud, Marx, Christ, and so on— to the furnace of his opinion. We sought Youth's opinion on every imaginable subject. What a reversal! "A professor," wrote Raymond Aron some years ago, "would have to be very ignorant indeed to be more ignorant than his students, particularly in their first years at university." But according to Youth, feelings were the energy of consciousness. He felt more than we did, so much so that verbalizing about it was, like, nowhere.

My friends aren't stupid. They had heard of est and Esalen, meditation and modern dance, More House and massage, Arica and acupuncture, hypnotism and health foods, tantric yoga and tai chi, Rolfing, Reich, Gestalt, biofeedback, Silva Mind Control, Fischer-Hoffman, Swami Raj-ji. That the brain had two hemispheres didn't surprise them. They wanted, however, to talk about the authoritarian component in the new therapies, the combination of Marine drill instructor and Mary Baker Eddy that was Werner Erhard. What, after all, about Sufism?

Youth, typically, shrugged. Could he, he asked, see the children? Our children had long since been shelved for the night. But Youth liked to rap with kids, who are the ears of Maya. And Youth as usual served himself, went upstairs. He was back in ten minutes with a bleary-eyed crew: "They want me to sing," he explained. How do you argue with vanilla ice cream? He unslung his guitar. We lit a candle.

Youth specialized in a medley of sixties songs—"Blowin' in the Wind," "We Shall Not Be Moved," "Let the Sun Shine," "Where Have All the Flowers Gone?," "Hey, Jude"—even though he had been two years old when the sixties started. He could have been singing about Easter, 1916, or Agincourt, or the burning of the library in Alexandria. Whereas my friends had been at

Berkeley, or in Mississippi, or thumped on by Chicago cops, before—with children and hotel reservations—we had marched on Washington by Metroliner.

What could we do? We sang along, and wept. Was it so shameful that we had gone by Metroliner to protest the war? Ought we forever apologize for private lives in which we sign our names as often on checks for worthy and unpopular causes as on petitions against this or that malfeasance? No. My friends weren't "into actualizing" themselves. They were fussing with the world. They made a distinction. Unhappy about the world, they would agitate; unhappy about themselves—well, they would change partners or jobs, go into analysis, drink too much, grapple with God in a dark alley, diet.

But the distinction was crucial. Whether or not feelings are the energy of consciousness, sometimes when you feel bad you ought to alter an institution or a policy instead of your consciousness. You ought to fiddle with social mechanisms instead of the oxygen flow to your brain. Werner Erhard to the contrary notwithstanding, on occasion everybody *should* feel bad, and a lot of other somebodies are at fault, and tinkering with the self amounts to criminal stupidity, and the new therapies add up to nothing more than those old magazine advertisements for techniques to improve your performance at the piano or in the bed—when the problem may not be music or sex or you. The problem may be political.

To Youth, one wants to say: Read a book, avoid California, don't take yourself too seriously, remember that children are easily pleased, that disappointment is an odds-on favorite to finish first, that honorable work is not to be sniffed at. We won't say this to Youth until after he has put down his guitar, because music is the sort of solvent that makes slush of generation gaps. And what we would really like to say to Youth is: You are lazy and inexperienced and self-righteous and naïve, and that perhaps is the only thing for which we can be properly blamed. We won't say these things of course, because if we didn't believe that Youth could improve on us, we would write novels about slitting our own throats. We feel sorry for Youth; he doesn't know any better, or the worst.

The Pampas

Because Dmitri acts before thinking, it follows that he is no stranger to remorse. The world punishes his sort of enthusiasm. The other Sunday night was a good example.

He invited friends over for popcorn and an opera. The opera had arrived by album in the mail from a public relations agency. Dmitri is one of those people whose names were stolen in their infancy and sold to Addressograph machines in strange places. Thus he is forever receiving form letters from Salvador de Madariaga, invitations to buy a summer home in surprising Samarkand, free books on astrology and stock fraud and complimentary copies of magazines devoted to fellatio.

At first glance, the opera looked as though it belonged in this category of the unwanted and the unnecessary. Either that, or it was a prank perpetrated by S. J. Perelman. Who else but S. J. Perelman could have imagined "an opera based on the life of Eva Perón, 1919–1952"? *Evita*, however, was serious, with music by Andrew Lloyd Webber and lyrics by Tim Rice. You will recall that Mr. Lloyd Webber and Mr. Rice were unindicted co-conspirators in the case of *Jesus Christ Superstar*.

The sheer unlikelihood of such an enterprise moved Dmitri to guffaw. After Jesus Christ, Eva Perón! What next? St. Teresa? Chairman Mao? Truman Capote? Well, no. Apparently one had to die young, in one's early thirties, to qualify for Rice and Lloyd Webber. With that impetuosity that has always disturbed his children, the cats and other pedestrians, Dmitri decided to listen to *Evita*.

Two hours later he was hung-over with chagrin. He *liked* *Evita*. It was, to be sure, a pastiche of pop-musical styles and bop-calypso, with a little bit of nineteenth-century bad breath blown in for giggles. But so in a way was Dmitri a pastiche, a disposable container for DNA. Like Dmitri, *Evita* sought to ingratiate. And when Eva Perón (Julie Covington) sang:

The Pampas

Don't cry for me, Argentina,
For I am ordinary, unimportant
And undeserving
Of such attention
Unless we all are—
I think we all are

Dmitri thought of the pampas. It had been a long time since Dmitri had thought of the pampas. In fact, he couldn't remember ever having thought of the pampas. "What's to think about the pampas?" asked the woman in his life. Dmitri summoned his friends.

About Dmitri, you must understand that for occasions he is sincere. He believes that civilization depends on ceremony. The shared event renews community, flirts with awe. His house is open for Election Nights and Super Bowls, Oscars and moon-landings. His house is open, it sometimes seems, whenever schools are closed. He solemnizes holidays, with ice cubes. And if there aren't enough occasions for ceremonies, he will invent some. He once gave a "Happy Birthday, Shakespeare" costume party, at which guests were supposed to be parts in the plays. A young woman wearing a clump of lettuce on her sleeve had offended him in his sincerity by explaining: "I am a Caesar salad, the noblest romaine of them all."

About Dmitri's friends, you must understand that they haven't been sincere since acne. They mainline on amused suspicion. "Are you putting me on?" they ask, as though they're afraid they'll fit. Their approach to music, politics, sadness, sex and sleep is oblique. Like shutters, they slant. They are looking for an angle. They are agnostic even on the subject of popcorn. They came to Dmitri's on Sunday night—their faces maps, their warts gleaming like jewels—because *Kojak* had been moved to Tuesdays.

About *Evita*, Dmitri's friends were heavily ironic for the half-hour they bothered to tolerate it. Where, they wanted to know, was Jorge Luis Borges? Borges should have booked and lyricked *Evita* as Lillian Hellman and Richard Wilbur had done for Leonard Bernstein's *Candide*. Why not operas on Pat Nixon, Rose Franzblau, Dita Beard and Mary Worth? Dmitri explained about dying young. Well, then, why not Marilyn Monroe or Simone Weil? They also suggested a musical version of Oswald Spengler's jeremiad, *How the West Was Lost*, with Tiny Tim as Weimar, Elizabeth Taylor as Socialism, Bette Midler or Sammy Davis, Jr., as the Reichstag fire and Rupert Murdoch as the Treaty of Versailles.

What they didn't do was listen. They were fizz machines; they sat there letting experience deposit itself, like a coin, in the holes in their heads, and then they made bubbles. They lacked, thought Dmitri, innocence. And one by one they deserted him for other rooms in the house, to talk of money and chew on drapes. Dmitri hadn't been so depressed since the night his children left town while he was watching himself on public television. His children, of course, had been right. So, perhaps, were his friends. Maybe his enthusiasm was nothing more than bad taste. He thought of good taste as an owl. Maybe his enthusiasm frightened owls.

When the woman in his life found him, after his friends had gone home, he had dimmed the living-room lights so low that the walls looked like bruises. "Hi, gaucho," she said.

"According to Boris Pasternak," Dmitri replied, "Nietzsche's principal function was to be the transmitter of the bad taste of his period."

"Well, you aren't Nietzsche. Besides, we've got TV to do that."

"I've never," he said, "gotten the point of irony. You strike an attitude, like a match, and it consumes itself. They hated *Evita*."

"They won't know what to think until they read a magazine."

"If you were a Total Woman, you would remove my socks, put peanuts between my toes, and nibble me insensible."

"I brought you Jack Daniels and an ice bucket, instead."

He regarded her: red hair and freckles. How was it that Russian Jews and Irish Catholics had monopolized red hair and freckles? Sincerely, enthusiastically, he said, "I have *excellent* taste." One advantage of remorse is that it sets the stage for consolation.

On Being Stupid

My father sang tenor, drank rye and died young. I was twenty-three years old at the time, and a continent away, and hadn't seen much of him since age eight. Relatives advised me of his death by wiring for some money to help bury him. My grandmother used to say he could have been another Dennis Day, on the radio. But he wasn't very good at life. I inherited his small bones, and whenever I am not being very good at life, when I am stuck in a procrastination that is actually a form of panic, I look at my hands and wonder if, like a recessive gene, his surrender is inside of me.

I remember standing in the control room of a radio station in Berkeley, California, with the telegram, trying to decide what expression to put on my face, what behavior to select. According to Freud, this was a significant moment in my life. We are so practiced in our self-consciousness that we've got it down to a disease. I was shopping for an appropriate emotion. What I bought was stupidity. To be stupid in front of the fact of death was, I thought, a kind of cleverness.

Some people weep, some drink, some keen, some platitudinize, some go to bed and don't get up for a while, some take charge and make telephone calls and arrangements. I get stupid. I haven't had to do so often. A few of us are tourists. Decade after decade goes by, and the worst we have to face are sprained ankles and disappointments. We go to hospitals because that's where children are born. Or we take our children to hospitals when they have concussions or pneumonia. (My son, for instance, is the one to whom concussions and pneumonia happen, as if he is being punished for his excellence. Maybe bad luck skips a generation.) Cats die. My friends went to graduate school instead of Vietnam.

There was one friend, six years ago, who was punished for his excellence. He was so good at life that we couldn't even bring ourselves to envy him. He edited a magazine. and wrote books, and ate and drank and smoked too much, and was the wittiest person I knew. But no one ever accused God of a sense of humor. He died on an operating table. I was called in the middle of the night, because it was known we were to publish an unfavorable notice of his new book in a magazine that had already gone to press. People wanted me to stop the print-run, as though a book review could possibly pertain to the larger unfairness. It was their way of being stupid in front of the fact of death.

For this friend, there was an elaborate memorial service. Diplomats and journalists attended, famous names said graceful things and a party followed. I suppose we were too scared not to have a party. By midnight, the friends of my friend were telling their favorite stories about him, repeating his best jokes, attempting impersonations. They had formed a circle, not a wailing wall, and passed around champagne, which they drank directly from upended bottles, as if they were characters in a novel of brave, doomed youth. I appreciate the theory of a wake, or an exorcism. Nevertheless, I put on my stupidity and went home.

This is not much of a dossier on death, is it? Thin. Hearsay. The telephone that rings in the middle of the night—nobody is calling to announce that you have won a lottery. You have always lost this lottery. My eyes are weak. When in the morning, not yet having put on my glasses, I go to the door to pick up my copy of *The New York Times* and see a banner headline, a black smear, I want to close the door and go back to bed and be stupid. Banner headlines in the morning *Times* are usually the same as telephone calls in the middle of the night: another Kennedy is dead.

I used to think that the Kennedys were dying—or going mad —for me, in my stead. They were using up all the available bad luck, the senselessness. It wasn't necessary to be stupid about the Kennedys: the networks would cope, and someone would sing "The Battle Hymn of the Republic," and everybody would write books, and you could go into the other room and count your children and they would still add up, and then it was all right to cry or be angry, to make fists with your brain, to throw up. You were safe, and didn't have to choose a behavior. The behavior would choose you.

Now, of course, another friend has died, on the tennis court, of a heart attack, at age forty-nine. It was not the birthday present I wanted. By definition, our friends are those people the world can least afford to lose. We are getting to be of an age when it is difficult to grow new friends; we haven't the energy, the time to cultivate; each one gone is a permanent impoverishment. We are also getting to be of an age when our friends are doing a lot of the dying; each one gone is a surprise, but the surprises now are more likely to arrive once a year than every six years or two decades. To deflect this bad news requires the sort of permanent stupidity even I am not clever enough to sustain.

He was, though, a particular friend, and particularly suspicious of the impulse to generalize. The best of editors, he demanded evidence. No train of thought was allowed without freight cars of facts. Fiercely honest—his friends were not spared—he would have been the first to admit that his poker-playing left much to be desired, he didn't know how to tell a joke and he couldn't carry a tune. He hated television. He loved food, tennis, truth and—because of a highly developed sense of the preposterous—frogs. He owned just one tie, which stayed in a drawer in the desk in his office, waiting for the publisher of this newspaper to convoke a solemn lunch. He would be wherever you were, when there was trouble. He wanted to be young again. Too briefly, he was.

His admirable sons, who have perhaps inherited his sense of the preposterous as I inherited my father's small bones, decided to bury him without a tie, in the tennis clothes he was wearing when the universe made a criminal mistake. There was, in the memorial rites last Thursday, a want of ceremony. Informality honored him. It occurs to me, however, that—in the clumsy way men in this country mismanage their emotions—I never got around to telling Al Marlens that I loved him. And so I thought that this time around I would be stupid in public.

On Being Excellent

Since we shall be devoting this solemn space next week to the terrors of being average, the sermon for this morning is on excellence, and what to do when—opening a refrigerator or an oven or a closet or a mind—you find it. Excellence sits there, like a rutabaga with edible tubers. It doesn't require you. In several ways, you are a threat to it. As it contemplates itself, you may be hungry, as we all are, for rainbows, approval, a second wind and a second chance, and you may settle for this rutabaga.

The consumption of excellence in our country, by people who really want something else, is a big problem. We try to take care of the problem with junk food and junk music and Merv Griffin, but some indiscriminate self in the middle of the night is always eating all the rutabagas, and then there isn't any excellence when we need it.

Let us assume, however, that you understand yourself to be more of a custodian, an encourager, of excellence, than a consumer; that in a way you are a talent scout for rutabagas in unlikely places. I'm not talking about excellence in the arts, and those critics who are supposed to be looking for it. The arts, with the help of the oil companies, will take care of themselves, and the critics are well paid for their dyspepsia. The arts, anyway, are always complaining. This space is reserved for the rhapsodies and lamentations of domestic life, the soft stuff inside the carapace of self. Let's say, then, that you're a teacher instead of a critic.

Some excellence came to our house the other day. The teacher in the family brought it home. I wasn't paying attention—I was in the columbarium, sharpening the teeth on my opinions—but this excellence had every reason to feel warm and secure. We are calm people hereabouts. We remove our shoes before taking showers. Excellence didn't exactly throb or anything. It just sat there inside its transparent plastic folder, one of a dozen or so term papers perpetrated by young ladies of fierce intelligence, all of whom will someday go to college and most of whom manage to look like Arab refugees, if Arab refugees wore Adidas sneakers before, during and after showers and jihads. Excellence was waiting for a grade.

That I should have found myself rummaging among the term papers of a group of sixteen-year-olds is perhaps enough of an astonishment to have caused someone to call a Sullivanian or the Royal Canadian Mounties. I don't want to be sixteen again; I'm sorry I was the first time. I never in my life want to take another test. If I didn't hate every school I went to—and there were a dozen of them—I've forgotten which one. Other people dream of falling and spiral staircases; I dream of orthopedic gym, Latin exams, the combination having been changed on my locker, losing my copy of *Silas Marner*. On bad nights, I am flotsam on a sea of formaldehyde, it rains carbolic acid and the Frog God is after me for having botched a dissection. Childhood is overrated.

But among the many things I am tired of these days—Idi Amin, Con Ed, articles on structuralism, people who obstruct the sidewalk demanding that I "check out" a massage parlor or a phrenologist—I am tired of watching the Knicks on television getting pushed around by teams from places like San Antonio and Indianapolis. San Antonio! They couldn't even win the battle of the Alamo. And so the other night I went upstairs to practice my snit, and there in gay profusion—actually, a mess—were the term papers, and I didn't feel like reading Lao-tzu, and so I rummaged.

Well, if I had been doing work like this when I was sixteen, maybe by now I'd be smart. There wasn't a dummy among them. But among them, singular and splendid, a sort of Adidas of term papers, was excellence: a challenging subject, a prodigious bibliography, original research, handsome prose, a happy way with quotes, bold calligraphy and strong thinking. This excellence could have adorned many a scholarly journal; it was missing from most of the books I review for a living. As always when the world has pleasantly surprised me, I whistled some Mozart and fixed a drink.

We come now to the first serious argument in a young marriage that has been mostly fire and ice cream. The teacher in our family meets with other teachers from her school to brood about grades. The school uses numbers, from 1 to 100, which finicky precision I find offensive to the human spirit and the plasticity of our nervous systems, besides being anal and arbitrary about degrees of value—how would I, numerically, grade my gene pool on a scale of Mozart?—but I am not yet your king. I hung around, trying to look supportive and tormented.

They went at it like a College of Cardinals that had run out of Italians. Certainly there was enough smoke. Suddenly I understood them to be discussing excellence. Surely, I croaked, you will give her 100? No, it seemed that was not sure. But wasn't this the best paper you have ever received or are likely to? That was agreed. Hasn't she fulfilled and exceeded your demands? Wouldn't you have been proud to have written this paper yourself? True, we guess. I mean, I don't even know the girl, but isn't she in a class by herself? Affirmative. Then *why*? We never give 100's. Why *not*? Nobody, they tell me, is perfect.

Does that, I wonder, include teachers, even the one I love enough to fluster a mongoose? Five points off for envy? If you have a scale of from 1 to 100, and excellence comes along, and you start talking about a 94 or a 95 or a 96, why don't you have a scale of from 1 to 96? The 100, I am informed, is an abstraction; the ideal can only exist by abstraction. Nothing is perfect.

A large point is being missed here, for which these teachers will be punished when excellence goes away to college and they are left with a bunch of 89's and shoes that pinch and rutabagas with poisonous tubers. All our lives, but especially at age sixteen, and especially if we almost deserve it, we want and need—for a moment or a single act of the intelligence and imagination, a performance—to be judged as perfect. Just once. Remember that term paper? It would make dying less of a cold surprise.

On Being Average

If you are accustomed, especially at airports, to thinking of other people as big trees among which your small children are lost, it comes as a surprise to see the head of your son—that shaggy beatitude—floating around at eye level. Did he just come off a rack instead of a plane? Stretched, or on stilts of bone, he ambles into his own future. Somebody watered his ankles, and overnight they elongated. He is only fourteen and it is suddenly clear that one day he will reach six feet. You never made six feet, not even on a chinning bar, and it doesn't look as though you ever will without a ladder.

You are, in fact, of average height, average weight, average speed and typical. Or is it nondescript? Nondescript means resembling nothing in particular. Typical means conforming to a particular type. You conform to a nondescript type. You should have been an embezzler or a spy. Going unnoticed is your style. It's as if your components were mass-produced, standard bland, like a slice of American bread or cheese. For you, spare parts, replacements, are always in stock. The ordinary, where you live, is despotic; an iron law of averages obtains.

Inside, of course, you seethe. The ego is a calliope. Let's say that once upon a time, when you were your son's age, a magazine photographer at school picked you to take a picture of. Ah, to be chosen! It tingled. You were confirmed in your splendid singularity. But why were you chosen, and for what? You were chosen, it was explained, because you seemed to be the typical American teen-aged boy.

There is no way to avenge this insult. It is the shadowy mugger in bad dreams. Try telling a magazine photographer that you are in no way typical; that you are peerless, and full of starlight, black holes, plankton, Monteverdi, Stephen Dedalus, minerals and jumping beans; that if you are regular, like a sonnet, you are also unique, like a Shakespeare. Just try it. It's like trying to tell your mother that yes, please, really, I *do so* have a sense of humor. You sound like a jerk.

To be regular, typical, bland, nondescript, standard, average is to be cursed. What are you, a Ramada Inn? You look in the mirror, and what you see is a study in inauspiciousness. You buy platform heels, and six days later you plummet down the subway stairs, where people walk around your body because they assume you're a pimp. You attempt a beard, and six weeks later you look like an undernourished armpit. Your hair starts falling out, and you remember what Cynthia Buchanan said of Norman Mailer: He combs metaphors over the bald spots on his theory.

But it is a theory of the self—yourself—that your body seems bent on disproving. Where, in the mirror or on the bathroom scale, is there any evidence of the self you want to be—flab of excess, scars of passion, fingerprints of the tender and the demonic? Will you die a Cub Scout? Are you, graded on the curve of life, a C student? When last seen, you weren't pumping iron or dunking basketballs. Is that why women kiss you on the cheek instead of the lips? One thinks of F. Scott Fitzgerald worrying about the size of his sexual organ. One thinks of Hemingway, who reassured him. Average.

Average! You know that there really isn't supposed to be any such thing. An average is an arithmetic mean, a quantity intermediate to a set of quantities. All over the place, there are deviations, inequalities.

In God's body shop, each of us was customized. But science came along to substitute statistical inference for free will. We are now a tribe of likelihoods, full of decimal points instead of jumping beans; our starlight's entropic. Helpless, blameless and boring, we'll try to win this one for the computer. You, Dmitri— an arithmetic mean, an intermediate quantity, a compost of likelihoods—have nowhere to hide. Once an average, always an average. The National Safety Council, the United States Bureau of Statistics, the March of Dimes and the Surgeon General even know exactly when you'll die.

Why doesn't it work both ways? If we are to be punished by

death for being average, why shouldn't those who are responsible for some of the deviations and inequalities that established this likelihood also be punished? If, for instance, you hit your son on the head with a hammer and he dies, you will at least face jail; in Utah, you would also face a firing squad and TV cameras.

If, on the other hand, someone sells dirty milk or poisons fish and the infant death rate goes up, he is merely fined. And if the American medical profession fails to reduce our infant mortality rate to the level achieved by Oslo in 1931, nothing happens to anybody at all.

How come the statistical correlation between two sets of events is truth in science and irrelevant in society? How come guilt isn't averaged? But you are sounding, again, like a jerk.

And here comes your son, and you haven't got a hammer, and you wish him gigantism, irregularity, deviation, spice, hair, guffaws, the moon and someone who can beat him at chess. He doesn't need your wishes. His will expands. At the collar and the cuffs, in the elbows and the shoes, he has outgrown his infant self. He is free to theorize. There is no average that he isn't above.

You seize a suitcase and hail a cab. The cab hails back. In his rear-view mirror, the driver looks at your inauspiciousness. "Don't I know you from somewhere?" he says.

"Unlikely," you reply.

"Wait a minute! Wait a minute!" he says. "Aren't you Bob Newhart?"

"Wrong," you explain. You are not tingling.

"I got it! I got it!" says the driver. "Wally Cox! Wally Cox!"

You are not amused. "Wally Cox is dead. He was excessive in Utah."

And then your son, the one with water on his ankles, leans forward and confides to the driver: "You really don't recognize him, do you? His name is Dean. John Dean."

Tinkertoys

In California, Dmitri thought of Wilfrid Sheed. On the face of it, that was ridiculous. The idea of California and the idea of Wilfrid Sheed are inconsistent, almost contradictory, like Uganda and Proust. But Mr. Sheed, a friend of Dmitri's who writes novels, wrote one once, called *Max Jamison*, in which this passage appears:

He was in love with the way his mind worked, and he was sick of the way his mind worked. The first thing that struck you about it, wasn't it, was the blinding clarity, like a Spanish town at high noon. No shade anywhere. Yet not altogether lacking in subtlety. Very nice filigree work in the church. This was the mind they were asking him to blow.

Dmitri would not have described his own mind as being anything like a Spanish town at high noon. It was more like Hong Kong or Shanghai before the war, cluttered and overcrowded, full of discrepancies and swamp gas. It was, nevertheless, the only mind he had, and in California they wanted to mess with it.

He went to California to present a paper at a symposium on "The Ambivalence of the Hickey in Fiction by Feminists Living Between Central Park West and Riverside Drive." Why is it that when John Kenneth Galbraith flies to California, he gets to sit next to Angie Dickinson, whereas when Dmitri flies to California he is manacled to a businessman who is mad at New York? The businessman was mad at New York because we won't let the Concorde stop here. If we let the Concorde stop here, for refueling, the businessman could make it from London to Los Angeles in five hours.

That people might fly against the clock from London to Los Angeles in five hours, giving them an extra day to do mischief, is one more compelling reason to shoot down any Concorde that gets anywhere near us. With slingshots and taxicab drivers, if necessary.

Tinkertoys

There was a car waiting for Dmitri in Los Angeles. This is because it is necessary in California to drive for two hours, whether
one wants breakfast or a chiropractor. Thus the illusion of progress
is sustained. For Dmitri, it was two hours north to Ojai, where golf
links lay like a rug in the lap of the mountains, God had arranged
for a squeaky-clean sky and bungalows festered. In California,
there is no last resort.

See the brave athletes hurl themselves at electric buggies and
drive—for two hours, of course—to the burning tee. See the tennis
courts, like runways for Concordes. See the swimming pool, a
sheet of undulant tin, around which are sprawled the idle and the
fricasseed. Why is everybody wearing linoleum? If God looked
down from his squeaky-clean sky, what would he think? They are,
in their crayon colors, expressing some deep sullen mystique of
abstract vapidity, some nonrepresentational fatigue.

Not for the first time, it occurred to Dmitri that leisure may
be a bad idea. Certainly leisure suits are. Seneca came to mind
before Wilfrid Sheed did: "Who has more leisure than a worm?"

As symposia go, this one went. If you've been to one plenary
session of a conference on how to improve the world, you've been
to them all. For his opinions, Dmitri was abused, and it was probably good for him. New Yorkers wear smarty-pants instead of
linoleum, and deserve an occasional kick in their surliness. It was,
however, in the workshops that they tried to mess with Hong Kong.

The workshops were really encounter groups. Each group had
a leader, only the leader was called a "facilitator." Dmitri's facilitator was a young man with kind eyes, a kind beard and kind
sandals, who spoke so softly that one wondered whether his pilot
light had gone out. Whatever one said to this agreeable person,
he'd reply, "Beautiful, just beautiful." And when everybody in
the group had said something, he'd sum up: "What I am hearing
a lot of in this room is . . ." And they *were* in a room, instead of
outside around a sand trap, because the beautiful things they said
a lot of had to be recorded on tape, and the microphone, like
God's necktie, hung from a squeaky-clean ceiling.

Dmitri was innocent of encounter groups. "Beautiful" was an
adjective he reserved for his wife, sunsets, Bach and Earl Monroe.

He was accustomed, moreover, when in small groups convoked for world-improving, to the white noise of gin and some pretzel nuggets. He was therefore astonished to be asked, while staring into his tenth Styrofoam cup of Styrofoam coffee, to describe his sex life.

Descriptions of his sex life he reserved for his wife and Bach. What was he supposed to say? "Very nice filigree work in the church"? If he wanted to make it public, he would write a novel, like the feminists and everybody else. But he didn't want to make it public, which seemed the direction in which the group was blundering, because the next proposal was that they get into some heavy touching.

Well. The idea was that one member of the group would close his or her eyes, and the other members would touch him/her, and he/she would try to guess whether the toucher was a he or she. Dmitri abstained. He no more wanted to be pawed by a bunch of strangers, however agreeable, than he wanted to reduce the music and mystery of love, the strange connection and the golden trust, to group chat, self-advertisement, anecdote. Next stop: the bathtubs of Esalen, which is not a Spanish town at high noon. He was urged to shuck himself of his inhibitions. What on earth for? He had spent most of his life acquiring them; inside their picket fence there was sanctuary, no microphones, a redeeming giggle. He imagined the polymorphs around a libidinal pool, ascertaining itch; off, then, with the linoleum, and let us go to water bed.

Are we Tinkertoys? A nice man at Ojai had spent an inordinate amount of time trying to come up with a nonsexist word to describe someone with whom you have a "significant emotional relationship." He arrived, after at least two hours of driving, at "attaché." So maybe we aren't Tinkertoys; we're luggage on a Concorde. Dmitri suggested, instead, "sidekick." No one was amused. And so, with his inhibitions and his sense of humor, he went home to a private life.

The Stoop

Standing on tiptoe, so as to appear in a towering rage, I shouted at them: "I laid my bones to, and drudged for the good I possess; it was not got by fraud, nor by luck, but by work, and you must show me a warrant like these stubborn facts in your own fidelity and labor before I suffer you, on the faith of a few fine words, to ride into my estate, and claim to scatter it as your own."

They replied: "*La propriété c'est le vol.*" (Property is theft.)

Well, that's not really what I shouted, nor what they replied. I don't quote Ralph Waldo Emerson before Vespers. They have certainly never even heard of P. J. Proudhon. And as for "a few fine words," the only ones they seem to know were popularized in the trenches of our various wars.

Here is the situation. I own a stoop. The stoop is attached to a house, and I am said to own that, too, meaning that I am a vassal in the service of a consortium of banks and credit unions, a motley of mortgages, Con Ed and the New York City tax assessor.

According to the tabloids, then, I occupy what's known as a "Manhattan townhouse." This suggests a sort of brownstone Deer Park, or a bunch of gout-ridden Whigs for a weekend of fox-flogging at the manse of Lady Elm Disease. It is actually eight small rooms, 13½ feet wide, piled two by two on top of one another. Inside, five people and three cats eat soybeans instead of dividend checks.

But I was talking about stoops. Because of television, stoops are no longer necessary. Having brought the sidewalk into our living room, we no longer require the variety of the street: the quaint drunks, the loose women, the ancient mariner and the occasional thug. We consult the horoscopes of ourselves. A stoop, which used to be the lower lip of our face on the neighborhood, is now vestigial, like an appendix or a sense of honor.

This is not to say that my stoop isn't still a crash pad. It is, though, a crash pad for strangers. There, on a summer night, the indisposed will doze it off. There, on a Sunday morning, sits the old woman with her sacks of Confederate money and MAC bonds. When the saps all rise each spring, lovers huddle on my stoop, rubbing their transistor radios. I sleep now at the back of the house, in order to listen to the exhaust fans of a restaurant specializing in stewardesses, but am obliged at least once a week to storm the local delicatessen. I find the flower box pillaged. Once, there was somebody's pet turtle. More often, there are locksmiths and Moonies.

Debris is one thing; *de trop* is another. It happens that my stoop is two blocks away from a junior high school. When the students are paroled for lunch, and it isn't snowing, they look for stoops. Mine, in the southern light off a diadem of trash basket, is apparently favored. There, squatting like Palestinian terrorists with Lone Ranger atomic-bomb rings, they unwrap themselves and revile each other. They are blind to the trash basket; it must be endocrinological. They are as trees in a permanent fright of autumn; they shed.

It is a striptease of straws and cardboard, of brown-paper bags and sleeves of pizza, bubble-gum leftovers and cigarette butts, the wayward pickle and the insolent bun and the incorrigible Cheez-It. They are slobs. I am not unacquainted with slobs, and I forgive more than most of my peer group has the time to grudge, but I draw the line at throwing soda-pop bottles on the pavement to see how far the shards will scatter, especially as I sit in a front room of my Manhattan townhouse reading Proudhon. Not only can't I concentrate, but I have also to clean up, or the Block Committee will cut off my allowance of ivy.

I have tried to reason with these scarlet pimples. Movingly, I spoke of the fouling of one's nest, reciprocity, the environment, John Rawls's *Theory of Justice*, the social contract and the Strategic Air Command. It was like trying to reason with the sullen pips on a stack of dominoes. Their resentment was made of bone. They resented even parting to permit me to descend to the street to mail the checks to pay off the interest on the loans that enabled me to buy the stoop on which they festered. Their convenience is some kind of Grail.

My son, an intermittent slob, has asked: "You always talk

about raising children. Why don't you talk about lowering them?" I remind him of Pascal: "That dog is mine, said those poor children; that place in the sun is mine. Such is the beginning of usurpation throughout the earth." My son scatters.

But usurpation is what it's all about. I am a middle-class liberal who feels so guilty about having gone into twenty years of debt to buy a townhouse that I can't even cope with the usurpation of a stoop by a swarm of slobs. I am apologizing to them for my working seven days a week to pay for enough space for five of us to have a place to hide. The stoops belong to the people. But maybe some people don't deserve the damn stoop, and I should be feeding them knuckle sandwiches instead of theories on the commonweal. Not by fraud, nor by luck, but by work, I ransomed this stoop. I'm willing to let anybody use it who treats it as if it were his own—a warrant of fidelity and labor. Am I supposed to provide ashtrays and diapers before I stop feeling that in some way it is my fault that people litter on my lower lip? Me, the grandchild of one of those best-selling Irish potato famines?

They animadvert on my origins. Being a middle-class liberal, I am of course nonviolent. There is, though, a faucet in the well beside the stoop, to which I've attached a garden hose. When they bomb my estate with soda-pop bottles, I will water down the stoop. This Ark comes with its own rain.

Baseball

When the news came to our silo last week that Mark "The Bird" Fidrych had torn a cartilage in his left knee and wouldn't be pitching for the Detroit Tigers for at least two months, I was on the roof, looking for low-level cruise missiles and trying to figure out the 1978 National Football League schedule. The National Football League schedule for 1978 seems to be a combination of a menu in a Szechwan sweatshop and the Code of Hammurabi. Is this good or bad for the SALT talks? What does Henry Jackson pretend to think? Or, more significantly, M. Donald Grant? If the Mets don't let the Nyets land Backfire bombers at Shea Stadium, will the Jets move to Vladivostok?

Meanwhile, down in the brig, my daughter had decided to play out her option, become a free agent and sign on next season with another father. My son wanted to renegotiate his contract. Both objected to limitations I had imposed on offensive strategic weapons and delivery systems after two broken lamps and an injured aunt. George Allen picked up my wife on waivers. Bowie Kuhn canceled my sale of the cats.

It wasn't the best of times. I felt as though someone had stepped on the crocuses. I felt like a New York Ranger.

"The Bird has been grounded," I told my spawn. They were playing soccer with the head of Evans and Novak. "I am reminded," I said, "of the Spruce Goose." They put Evans and Novak back into its column and plugged the Pentagon leak. Who was Spruce Goose? "Spruce Goose," I explained, "is the huge plywood seaplane constructed by Howard Hughes during the Second World War in Long Beach, California. Wingspan, 320 feet. Length, 219 feet. East Basin, Pier E. Although it is one of the largest planes in the world, it has been airborne only once."

They understood what I meant. Mark "The Bird" Fidrych is one of a kind, the only baseball player left in America for whom

I'd cross the street and tip my mitt, excepting maybe Luis Tiant. At life, all of us are rookies, and most of us can't hack nine innings. As 1976's American League rookie of the year, The Bird specialized in complete games. He also specialized in joy. He was, on the mound, a tuning fork; the acoustic space was full of good vibrations.

There are no good vibrations in a multiple independently targetable re-entry vehicle. Does Edward Teller talk to a MIRV, the way The Bird talks to a baseball? No. I resort to sports to take my mind off things like warheads and launchers, "throw-weights" and "bargaining chips." The brain needs waste space, a rumble seat, a DMZ. Other people play chess, read mysteries, do crossword and jigsaw puzzles, listen to punk rock, knit and masturbate. I go to ball games or watch them on television.

But they have filled up my waste space now with sullen millionaires, plutocratic crybabies, overpaid blabbermouths, tall men in their underwear who can't set a pick, .235 home-run hitters who can't catch a fly ball to the outfield, halfbacks who won't block because they're saving their profiles for TV commercials, gangsters on ice skates, brats with tennis rackets, armed goons and deferred performances. They live in tax shelters instead of dugouts, on the margin instead of the sideline. They warm debentures. They deserve Howard Cosell.

I love baseball—the artfulness in its pauses, its hesitations; the grace in the spaces of its waiting. Time does not apply. Whereas football hates the clock, a baseball game can theoretically last forever, like the SALT talks. Fifteen years ago, as a Dodger fan stranded in San Francisco, I couldn't raise Los Angeles on the radio inside my apartment. So at night after dinner I would pull the car out of the garage onto the sidewalk, yank up the aerial, guzzle beer and listen to Vince Scully, as if to civilization reporting from a distant star. There was no point in going to Candlestick Park; at Candlestick Park, they booed Willie Mays. The definition of the sticks is a town that boos Willie Mays.

Willie Mays, Stan Musial, Ted Williams, Roy Campanella: who the hell does Dave Kingman think he is? Henry Kissinger? MIRV Steinbrenner? Ozymandias? Please explain Graig Nettles.

Sparky Lyle isn't fit to wear Joe Black's jockstrap. Once upon a time the low-level cruise missiles were line drives, and a first strike wasn't preemptive. Now a bunch of stiffs on television sell panty hose, yogurt, banks, coffee machines, rental cars, telephone companies, hair sprays, atomizers full of something that smells like the guts of a sperm whale and their own dimples.

With The Bird grounded, my son wanted to know, does this mean you won't go to a game this summer? That's what it means, I lied. I will end up belly-flopping in the Kranepool; at least he knows how to hit to the opposite field. But why should I go to Yankee Stadium when the New York Stock Exchange is closer? How come the sports pages are just as depressing as the front page? That Thurman Munson feels bad because he isn't as pretty as Carlton Fisk is Thurman Munson's problem, not mine. And it wouldn't have occurred to Campanella as something to worry about. Don Gullet will make more money in the next three years than my mother will have made in a nine-to-five lifetime, and she's a better person than he is by a megaton.

Listen, I said to my son, you remember years ago when you kept telling me for weeks how well you were doing in baseball at school, and I kind of doubted it because a great athlete you're not, but you were a talking box score and finally I believed you and then one night you couldn't sleep for crying, and you were crying because you had made it all up, you weren't even on the team, you had lied because you thought it was important and you couldn't live in the same bed with the lie, unlike, say, a Pentagon, and I said baseball isn't that important, it isn't worth one of your tears, do you remember?

He did.

For once, I said, I was right.

The Power Party

It will happen by accident. No one will have warned you. Why should they? They have their own erotic depths and nasal passages to worry about. You will leave the safety of your typewriter, the sanctuary of your home—and perhaps a provocative book, only half read, on genetic engineering or how to process cannabis in a Cuisinart. Going out is a way of not watching *Scenes from a Marriage* on public television. What you expect is an unlacing of the mind among loose friends. Off with the boots of duty! Let us talk small, gnaw chicken and risk a giggle.

But this is not to be. You know it is not to be at the door of your friend's apartment, which is opened by one of those servants rented for the evening from a bat cave in surprising Queens. He will hide your raincoat, sneer at your blue jeans and fetch you a drink. It is, then, a serious party. At serious parties, New Yorkers are not expected to fetch their own drinks; having to move from one side of a room to the other would cramp us in our seriousness.

On the other hand, batpeople tend to pin you into conversational corners. You can't, when some aggressive gnome starts in on psychoanalysis or astrology, excuse yourself to freshen your drink. The fresh drink materializes at your elbow, like a character defect.

Nor are you able to employ what is known in select circles as the Michael Arlen gambit. The Arlen gambit is to arm yourself at the bar with a couple of your own drinks. Two-fisted, then, you can make your escape from any ambush by maniacal bores: "I'm sorry, I really would like to hear more about the basic engram and operating thetanism, but Duchess Pittsburgh is waiting for her toddy of goat's bile." (It is, to be sure, a tricky gambit for smokers. Both hands occupied, what are you to do with the burning weed in the middle of your food hole? If only ears had thumbs.) A batperson isn't going to fetch you two drinks at the same time, not unless he steals your ashtray.

You allow your eye to graze on the pasture of those present, and your bonhomie evaporates.

Can celebrityhood be said to glower? As if behind sandwich boards advertising their own famous names, they sit on sullen stools. It is wall-to-wall pout. See the famous TV anchorman, the famous magazine editor, the famous newspaper columnist, the famous courtesan. There are several novels, a Broadway play, half a Cabinet, two banks, one football team, a jazz musician and an Englishman. They are waiting for the latest edition of themselves, for the reviews, for an energizing principle.

There are too many celebrities and not enough sycophants. Such a discrepancy will be hard on the husbands and wives of the illuminati. Somebody has to grovel and sigh. Somebody has to be shouldered aside so that oaks may huddle before they're felled. This is more than serious. This is power, baby. This is the sort of party where you have to decide whether you are important enough to wait for the other fellow to say hello, or you have to say hello to the other fellow first.

Careers, like camels, hunker down to snooze with a wary eye on which way the fan is blowing.

You have been here before. It is always a mistake. It was a mistake three years ago, schlepping out to the Hamptons because you had never been there before, and how unworldly it was not to have seen the famous artists and writers behaving like debauched gazelles. And so you ended up in Sag Harbor as an uninvited guest at a stranger's birthday party, for which they imported Bobby Short.

Upon you they laid lobster and a grape of France and a What's-your-angle, sapajou? For yourself, you apologized. For the fifteen minutes they were famous, they famed and famed and famed. We end up, as Kurt Vonnegut has said, licking the boots of psychopaths.

The sad fact is that, taken singly, celebrities are interesting; in herds they low. It is a collective goiter; you want to give them a pill to reduce the swelling. Why are they driven to perform? In our art and science, the magic of our money-making, our sneaking politics, we adumbrate and counterfeit. A self is suggested. An image is projected.

Our children know better, but what a burden it is to pretend to be what we have made, to try to live up or down to an idea of us arrived at in some committee meeting or in desperation. It was, after all, just one idea among many.

What a trial to be Norman Mailer, Billy Carter, Farrah Fawcett-Majors; to have to grow a personality along the lines of the one you invented, the one that sold; to have to compete with other fabricated personalities, inflations of cunning, blimps of ego; to jostle at a power party. The more one distends, the more easily one is bruised. Friends would have forgiven you, instead of expecting a performance. You should have stood in bed, buttering your toast.

Suppose you are not clever, except at a typewriter. Suppose you are not sensitive, except in the middle of the night a month later. Suppose your generosity is theoretical, your courage wholly literary, your fast ball lacking jumping beans, your heartbreak is psoriasis. Suppose, deep down, you suspect that you are dull, and your public works are a form of vengeance. You talk a good poem, and think by numbers. Once upon a time, you were interesting; then Mother died and you had to give it up.

Friends ought to know who you really are, and invite you to dinner anyway. It needn't be served in a room where the walls are always white, the steel always stainless, the chicken always two hours late and the children stuffed into some hamper. Nor need it be oversubscribed with by-lines who deep down in the Cuisinart feel just as fraudulent as you do, who do not at dawn presume to be wise. There is no wisdom; there are only punch lines.

Communities

When a friend called to arrange a softball game, Dmitri was listening to WBAI. (Alfred Kazin asks in a letter, "Dmitri, Dmitri, why
always Dmitri? Why not Alyosha or Smerdyakov?" These are good
questions.) WBAI, for those of you who have been off on a cru-
sade to recover the Holy Land, is the listener-supported, noncommercial Pacifica radio station in New York City. There are also
Pacifica stations in Washington, Texas, Los Angeles and Berkeley,
California.

WBAI has been having its problems. Pacifica stations are always having their problems—with the Federal Communications
Commission, the Senate Internal Security Subcommittee, the listening audience, the staff, the transmitter, bomb-throwers and
witches. We won't go into WBAI's particular problems here because, on the whole, it would be easier to explain what's going on
in Zaire and, anyway, they have nothing to do with Dmitri's private life.

Happenstantially, the last time Dmitri had played softball on
a regular basis was also the time he had been working as a pro-
gram director for the Pacifica radio station KPFA, in Berkeley.
This was back in the Pleistocene epoch, when John F. Kennedy
was President of the United States. Not that the radio people,
except for Dmitri, played softball; they were always in the control
room, playing with reels of tape. But the graduate-student people,
Dmitri's friends from college days, would gather every Sunday
afternoon in Strawberry Canyon with bats, gloves and picnic
hampers.

These had been Dmitri's two communities. The graduate-
student people were for the most part indentured servants to the
social sciences, and looked to the sun to bake Max Weber out of
their systems. The radio people were for the most part temporary
dropouts from the white middle class; they went to radio instead

of graduate school. KPFA let them be graduate students of themselves—took them off the street and gave them machines and the ether to play with. The night itself seemed a benign ear.

If graduate-student people knew exactly where they were going—out of Parsonsian Functionalism into the dramaturgy of Erving Goffman or the ethnomethodology of Harold Garfinkel or the social exchange of George Homans—the radio people did not and did not care. KPFA was a shipboard romance, somehow parenthetical. There would be time, later on, for a career. Now was being young and left wing in northern California, a sort of permanent February when spring comes to the Berkeley hills.

In which hills there was softball, haphazard and coeducational. If the couples weren't married, they soon would be. And if there were children, they were tiny, strapped into strollers or tethered to a tree. Dmitri's son, six months old, napped with his head in a catcher's mitt, dreaming of Mazda knows what; artichokes, maybe. After the game, there always seemed to be beer and artichokes and, if one remembers correctly, Edith Piaf on a jukebox.

Nostalgia causes tooth decay. Or, as Vladimir Nabokov has observed, "The future is but the obsolete in reverse." Even California couldn't last forever. The community of Sunday softball players disintegrated abruptly. One Sunday—could Mazda or Smerdyakov please explain why?—serious athletes joined the game. It was important for them to make the double play. The following week more of them showed, wearing cleats. The week after that, they complained about the women, who struck out or popped up too often and missed the cut-off throw for the relay to the plate. A month later in left field, where of course a Pacifica radio person ought to have been, Dmitri looked around; no women, no children, no fun. Stuff this. He mounted his second-hand Vespa and left Strawberry Canyon forever.

Whereas the community of radio people just went away, one by one, to compose music, edit magazines, teach literature, direct movies, be adult, while nobody was noticing. And one day it was as if the Pacifica artichoke had been stripped down to its transmitter. Dmitri himself was last seen by Berkeley heading for the New Hampshire woods to write a novel not even his brother would want to read.

Yet Pacifica abides: which is why Dmitri was listening to WBAI when his friend called. *Collier's, Life,* the *Saturday Evening Post,* the *Herald Tribune,* the Bicentennial, the double standard, the fifty-dollar tax rebate and Bernardine Dohrn have vanished, but Pacifica radio abides. It must be needed. Is it having any fun? It would not seem so. It seems instead a snarl of factions, a nest of sects, a sword in the ear. It sounds like cleats.

In the 1960's, when the serious athletes took over the country and played Vietnam, everything—cars, trees, science, sex—got politicized. On the opposition team, Pacifica seems to have stopped making jokes. Surliness chairs the meeting; a resolution against giggles was approved by the subcommittee on correct thinking; gentleness got stomped on. A kind of linoleum of sound, a flat shriek, takes over: instead of discussion, fierce blurbs; instead of nuance, sirens. Do they listen to one another or, having recorded their alarms, do they go home and listen merely to themselves, like Mr. Nixon? Dmitri suspects the latter, which saddens him, because the rest of radio is either the Top Ten Tunes since the Renaissance or punk rock.

This is where we're supposed to wrap it up with some sort of epiphany. I'll try. For his son—that noncommercial transmitter, that dreaming artichoke, Alyosha at age fourteen—Dmitri wishes softball games played without cleats, and friends to arrange them, and communities to sustain them, parentheses and Pleistocene epochs and some dramaturgy. For his daughters, he wishes the same. We will find out this weekend whether the wishes of love abide.

The Support System

Just to survive in this city, we need a support system. It is the net and the trampoline, the singing booth and cloister, a wildlife refuge. It consists, of course, of friends, the people we can call in the middle of the night when the gods have dealt us a karate chop or the discrepancies seem to be gaining on us. Listen: they are raining on my parade, there's a microphone in my flowerpot, the elevator doesn't stop here anymore, Mozart died. According to the Irish, "What a friend gets is not lost"—a proverb I take to have several meanings.

But this support system consists as well of things, about which we are superstitious, and of services, upon which we are dependent, and of routines, by which we limber up the mind for vaulting. An exchange of energies, a movable magic, is involved. The material world throbs with portents. And grudges. A trusted tool, a favorite poem, a Judy Collins record, an all-night delicatessen, the school bus, the mailman, the traffic light and a liquor store that cashes checks are necessary to my well-being. If any one of them fails me, I am up angst creek without a paddle; I am down in the lumpen. For example:

Accustomed as I am at seven o'clock in the morning to finding fifty-seven sections of *The New York Times* at my door, if *The New York Times* is missing I fear and tremble. There will be no weekend; homeless, how is one to go on living? Denied my morning print-fix, I read the writing on the wall: "I am poured out like water, and all my bones are out of joint: my heart is like wax; it is melted in the midst of my bowels" (Psalms 22:14). On opening the refrigerator I disclose, instead of orange juice, Anita Bryant.

There is reason to believe that my support system needs new shock absorbers. Consider the neighborhood bar and the coffee bean.

Neighborhood bars are for cronyism. Cronyism is a suburb of

the support system. We go there to nod and hoot like owls in a mirror—a garden—of bottles, above which inflated nymphs cavort. The TV set, the moon, is in some phase of baseball game. The afternoon itself is a complaint. Dry heads eat Wise potato chips.

And the neighborhood bar is disappearing. It is being elbowed off the avenues by singles joints, service stations of the libido. Waiters dressed like rugby hoodlets bring cinders of beef and buckets of fizz to blank bodies in search of thumbprints, while, on the jukebox, six synaptic clefts sodomize an electric bathtub.

This isn't my idea of cronyism.

Journalists, especially, need neighborhood bars. We need a place to contemplate the anatomy of our editors, and to devise new uses for old organs. One cable on our support system is the gripe. They are raining on our gripe. The bars are falling down all over Times Square.

We used to go to Schrafft's on Forty-third Street, until they leveled it to make another movie house. We tried Sun Luck on Forty-fourth; it neglected to pay its taxes, and is dark now; the chicken wings and spare ribs no longer talk to one another. We moved back to Forty-third and Stefano's, until they ripped out the bar to make more room for tables. For the moment, until the discrepancies catch up with us, we slog through Shubert Alley to Barrymore's, on Forty-fifth, to see which actors are out of work and to consort with Mira.

In Restoration England, Mira would have been called a barmaid. Actually, she sings, and maids bar at Barrymore's while waiting for her break. And, in fact, you can tote your bale this evening to the Felt Forum to hear and see her sing or you can hibernate until May 15th, when the show hits public television. I wish her all the luck she doesn't need because she's very good, and yet . . .

She is going to vault, on the pole of her talent, out of our lives. She is going to disappear, like Schrafft's. She is going to ride away, like Shane. The support system starts to unravel. The rough beast of me slouches toward Barrymore's on matinée day; my cave is overgrown with theater parties, leisure suits, opera glasses, twitter.

I hack my way to the bar hoping to find Mira, and see instead a sign: NO COFFEE.

Now this is portentous, an Anita Bryant. For about a month, Barrymore's has been charging a dollar for a cup of coffee in an attempt to discourage customers from playing into the greedy hands of the Brazilian bean kings. Apparently it hasn't worked, and so radical action has been decided on: NO COFFEE. The sign has the purity of an abstraction, the clarity of Euclid. It does not apologize for itself. It is final.

Unlike Mira, coffee is an acquired taste. We have nevertheless acquired it extravagantly. To be sure, we have been warned, by the people who edit our days and nights, that coffee is bad for us. I am tired of being warned. These are the things I have been warned against in the last three years:

Paint, detergents, birth-control pills, intrauterine devices, aerosol cans, hair dyes, hair sprays, eye drops, Pacemakers, antiperspirants, amphetamines, tranquilizers, asbestos, vinyl chloride, monosodium glutamate, microwave ovens, evaporated milk, artificial sweeteners, breakfast cereal, sandwich spreads, peanuts, pasta, strawberries, swordfish, mushrooms, bacon, eggs, tea bags, beer, aspirin, marijuana, antacids, pesticides and X-rays, not to mention cigarettes and alcohol, and not to think about Ralph Nader.

Why should laboratory rats have all the fun?

Life causes cancer.

I can do without most of the things I have been warned against, plus Arab oil. I do not see, though, how I can do without coffee and Mira at the same time.

Suckers

If you were at the Felt Forum last Wednesday night, as I instructed you to be, you would have noticed that Mira, the singing barmaid, was not. There or singing. In the history of evil and disappointment in our city, this is merely a footnote. But most of us are merely footnotes, and maybe if we got together there would be enough of us to crawl over the face of one of those big people who do all the laughing. I dream so.

Here is how it worked. A producer came into Barrymore's one night, along with a guy who plays piano. The producer had heard Mira sing in one of the clubs. He was putting together a show at the Felt Forum, and he wanted her. The piano player, who has a good reputation, would be her accompanist. It also looked as though WNET, Channel 13, would tape the proceedings.

This, of course, is the sort of break in whose existence a young performer must believe in order to stay out of the bottle or Bellevue. While not a lot of money was involved, it beat knocking on doors all over town trying to get into a television commercial. It meant exposure. And the producer would spring for a couple of gowns, which Mira would choose and be allowed to keep.

Somehow or other, Mira ended up investing fifty dollars in the show. Just because you're talented doesn't mean you think like David Hume when good luck seems to have laid its sword on your shoulder.

Anyway, there were details to pin down, papers to sign, Mira would have to get her charts copied for the accompanist. That costs money, but the producer would do it for her. She gave him the charts—the arrangements for her songs—and a portrait to use for publicity purposes, and went off to select her gowns.

For about a week there, Barrymore's was a very pleasant place to be. Happiness is contagious. Through binoculars of shotglass, we perceived the world as just. It is as if you sit in the tree of your talent; that tree has been bent back, wired toward the ground by circumstance; someone happens along and snips the wire; you are catapulted into the wondrous strange.

I remember years ago collecting rejection slips from publishers and magazines who didn't want my novel or my articles. The room where I worked had a walk-in closet, which I papered with rejection slips. I stapled them where I could see them every morning before I sat down at the typewriter. Is this what Robert Ornstein means when he speaks of "tantrum yoga"? It certainly maddened my prose. When at last somebody bought the novel, I invited friends over and burned the rejection slips in the back-yard barbecue rotisserie. I was up there so high in the ozone layer that the blood in my brain boiled.

Like that. Only, the producer disappeared, with Mira's charts, her portrait and her fifty dollars. The store called to say that he hadn't signed for the gowns, and did she still want them to do the alterations? Messages left at his hotel were unavailing. Felt Forum was feeling uncommunicative. It is a long way down from the ozone layer. It stings, too.

As scams go, this one seems far too elaborate for a fifty-dollar payoff. Aren't there easier ways to steal that much money? Ways that don't require the moving around of so much paper? Why not smash parking meters instead of dreams? Maybe the producer himself is a dreamer, and a deal dropped dead on him, and he's embarrassed. All right. Give her back her charts. Arranged in her key, they are of no use to anyone else, and she will just have to pay her arranger to do them over again. We'll give him a week.

And as scams go, this one is small change in the larger scheme of rip-offs. It lacks the daring, the grandeur, of General Motors—putting Chevrolet engines into Buicks, Oldsmobiles and Pontiacs. It lacks the magnificent disdain of the New York Telephone Company—which hasn't bothered to advise its customers of the existence of its least expensive class of service. It's not like buying an Italian general or a Japanese political party or a Latin-American republic. It's merely your ordinary, everyday indecency.

I wonder if the producer is sitting around somewhere with Mira's charts on the couch I bought from Oliver last summer? These people aren't even big enough to qualify as bandits.

But we are prisoners in suckerdom. Having been had, our understanding of ourselves is narrowed. We internalize the blame: sucker. The way of the world is our fault because we permitted ourselves to believe that the way of the world was nicer: klutz. It will be necessary from now on to squint, or not look at all, when the shamans show up with their spirit water: wooden nickel. Get wise; life is fixed; on the margin of the sly, no flies on me: bumpkin, tenderfoot, mooncalf, yokel. We accuse ourselves of what was best in us, and crystallized cynicism is the residue.

Not much to sing about, is it, at Felt Forum or anywhere else.

I would miss the yokel in me; he is a better person than the cop, the shyster, the commissar and the crybaby who sometimes seize control of my console and bulldoze the gentle possibilities of each brave new day in the imperial city. The mooncalf does the singing. On his or her behalf, then, let's put the angry prophet or the scourge temporarily in charge. Wrath cleanses: not wrath directed at ourselves for having dreamed foolishly, but wrath for the thieves of our pride and longing, the ragpickers and paperhangers and junkmen who leave stones in the mouths of the singers.

Sir, I Exist

Archie Bunker came into our lives the other morning in an airport bar. It was, of course, too early to be drinking, and in fact nobody really wanted a drink, but travel is a temporary license to shoot breezes and kill time. Like the credit card, travel permits us to multiply our disappointments. And if, in San Francisco, they open the airport bar at ten o'clock in the morning, somebody has to go in. We might have been on our way from Riyadh to Rangoon. I often think so.

Anyway, loud and thick, he looked like a Bunker who had lost his Norman Lear. Whatever we had been quietly discussing— basketball or quarks, I forget which—was trampled under. From Suzy, who was tending bar and whom he called "cutie," he demanded rye. From the rest of us, he demanded attention. He had feelings and opinions: on how beautiful it was in California, on how cold it got at Candlestick Park, on how much he needed to relax, on how far he had to travel, on airplanes and dungarees and money and his brother.

One by one we slipped away, fugitives from noise.

He followed; no long gray beard, but a glittering eye. It burned its way, in the passenger lounge, through the newspapers behind which we were trying to hide. Hey, where you from? Where ya goin'? Whaddaya think of the weather out here? Not bad, not bad. What time ya got? He was an Ancient Mariner without a secret. Maybe he was looking for an albatross to talk to death.

I put on my anonymity. It is the latest in anonymities, safari bush-style, monochromatic, with a hood and epaulets. I wear it on subways and in Times Square. It failed to dissuade him. He knew I was in there. We would be winging to New York together.

In my experience, to be seated in the smoking section of the coach compartment on the port side of an American Airlines DC-10 is to be ignored by stewardesses, or flight attendants, as they now characterize themselves. The wine bottle never comes back your way; the coffeepot is suddenly empty; the only attractive entrée on a dinner menu otherwise devoted to sludge has been gobbled up.

I'm sorry, sir; first-class nonsmokers ate all the Aztec virgin hearts. Would you like Ovaltine with your sludge?

Why this is so, I don't know, any more than I know why Otto, turned inside out, spells "toot." It is nevertheless a fact. There's a poem by Stephen Crane I must paraphrase because I can't find it. A man says to the universe: Sir, I exist. To which the universe replies: That, sir, does not inspire in me a sense of obligation. In the larger scheme of DC-10's, the flight attendants are the universe.

One maunders. Well, you could have cut my dismay with an alpenstock when I found that not only had I been consigned, once again, to Coventry, but that the Archie Mariner was right behind me. Next to me, mercifully, was a student of the Bible in Portuguese. The books, magazines, headphones and blindfolds with which I adorn myself on flying, just in case the computer has mated me with an Englishman who spent some time in India, were therefore unnecessary.

But the Archie Mariner was immediately aft, a lumbar mouth. After having to be reminded to buckle his seat belt, he monitored our takeoff.

Because he had forgotten his watch, this required his demanding to know the time every two minutes. (Once we were up, it was every fifteen minutes.) He fussed. When big men fuss, mice get ulcers. Had they turned off the no-smoking sign? Yes, we admitted. He wanted some rye to relax him. Later, explained the universe. He needed to move around, meaning that he grabbed my seat-back to hoist himself and, on releasing it, slung me toward the cockpit. When appetizers arrived, he wanted dinner. When dinner arrived, he wanted heart of Aztec virgin. When cordial arrived, he wanted his eighth little bottle of rye. When we touched down at Kennedy, he was off and running while we taxied the usual twenty minutes to the gate, and had to be restrained.

I should emphasize two things. First, he unfailingly apologized to everybody every time he bothered them. Second, he bothered everybody all the time.

During those five and a half hours, I learned from the Archie Mariner that he had been in California for a week to visit his sick brother; that the climate out there was terrific; that he'd come out on a 707, which wasn't as relaxing as this DC-10; that the "elements" had taken over New York, especially midtown Manhattan where he delivered mail for a living; that he had paid for his dinner and therefore had a right to Aztec virgin hearts; and that maybe in two years he'd have another chance to visit California and pamper his niece.

I learned this because he repeated it obsessively. Athwart the restrooms, he had a captive line. Having used up the patience of the universe, he made sure the rest of us smoking-coach cirrhosed livers wouldn't get a plastic fork to stir the salt in our Ovaltine. You couldn't get near him without hearing all there was to him. To the vicinity, he loudly confided. He seemed to be saying that he had no secrets, and we thought he probably didn't.

Then why, on our landing at Kennedy, were there tears in his eyes?

Because it must have been his first coast-to-coast round trip, or he would have known how to behave himself. Because there would be no one to meet him, or he would have mentioned a wife or child. Because the excitement, the singularity, of this flight opened up an eagerness in him to spill, prolong and ratify his emotions, to connect with his experience. Because there is an establishment, of the air—college students, businessmen, vacationers, refugees, with parents or expense accounts—and an etiquette of the air, a numbness composed equally of acquiescence and condescension; and a snobbism of the air. Only kids are allowed to be weepy or enthusiastic. The Archie Mariner gave us everything he had; we hoarded. Up in the air is upper class, even if it's not first. He wanted to hold on to what we wanted to get over with.

Sir, he said to the universe, I exist. Believing him would have been inconvenient. It might even have inspired a sense of obligation.

The Garden of Schopenhauer

It was not, admittedly, adult behavior. In fact, he closed the door on the room full of modern novels, and, in the hall, turned Schopenhauer's face to the wall. There had been afternoons when he consoled himself by thinking about Schopenhauer's having consoled himself by thinking about the Upanishads, but this wasn't one of them. He climbed the stairs to the kitchen and fixed his first gin-and-tonic of the season. In the past, his first gin-and-tonic of the season had invariably caused snow to fall for another six weeks, but he thought that God was probably preoccupied these days with Jimmy Carter and wouldn't notice.

He had been out in the neighborhood, to buy tonic water and rescue some shirts from the Cultural Revolution on the corner. The talk in the neighborhood had been about the bust of the after-hours gambling casino across the street. The talk had then gone on to which nearby Italian restaurant laundered money for what we used to call the Mafia before they passed a resolution against calling the Mafia the Mafia. Meanwhile, there was apparently a female bookie just a block away.

In his neighborhood, where men still got haircuts and all the travel agencies advertised charter flights to Budapest, everybody noticed everything, and what they missed they made up. The antique stores and barbershops were factories for scandal.

On the street, he had contemplated his house, his sanctuary. Ever since he had published a tantrum, the junior high school students kept the stoop clean, thus blowing on the embers of his faith in the plasticity of the human nervous system. A real estate agent had told him that buying a brownstone in this city is often the last act in the melodrama of a failing marriage. Surely debt, if not children, would keep a couple welded to each other. When it does not, brownstones all over town are occupied by women and children, while men sleep on refrigerated Hide-a-Beds in the apartments of distraught friends. Why is it that real estate agents only sound like Schopenhauer *after* they've made a sale?

No, not this time. His house was his gambling casino, and he had rigged it to win. The plumbing now obliged. The cats, bored with bothering him, were rolled up like pairs of Argyle socks in a puddle of sunshine under the skylight. The new couch abided, like a Haitian white canoe waiting to be paddled across the living room. His children had sober friends and good grades. Excellence, after all, had been given 100 on her term paper. Even *Evita* was going to be made into a movie, although he had always missed the point of Ann-Margret.

According to Schopenhauer, "A woman represents a sort of intermediate stage between a child and a man." Schopenhauer, sadly, had never met the woman of this house. She cried only on thinking about Trotsky. Even now, she was teaching internal con-tradictions to the daughters of the ruling class. Schopenhauer probably spent his whole life sleeping on refrigerated Hide-a-Beds.

And what of him, our Indian, listening in the kitchen to the vital organs of his house breathe, gliding in sweat socks and Mozart T-shirt, with a gin-and-tonic, through chancels of sunlight and birches of books, looking of course for an Upanishad? How would he stack up, according to a Schopenhauer?

"Man," said Schopenhauer, "is a burlesque of what he should be." Tell it to Mozart. But even Schopenhauer was sometimes right. It is hard to be an American male; we keep tripping over our wooden swords. We know, in our sweat socks, that we aren't deerslayers, whaling captains, river pirates, Lone Rangers, private eyes, Hemingway or John Galt. But neither, necessarily, are we Babbitts, Snopeses, organization pigs in gray flannel T-shirts, Daddy Megabucks. We should be allowed our sneaky dignity, the surprise of pride.

It occurred to him, going down the stairs, that he had not recently betrayed a confidence or a colleague. He was reminded that he made his living writing about books, that he was paid to read, to form opinions and to transcribe them; and that while this was peculiar, it wasn't sinful. The mailman, who had the most to complain about, forgave him: "Eat paper, drink ink," said the mailman (after Shakespeare). Or: "Here's another sepulchre of thought" (after Longfellow).

He wondered if, on thinking about mailmen, Schopenhauer would have been consoled.

There was a garden. Only a New Yorker would consider it a garden. To the untutored eye, it resembled a crater, as if Albania had attempted a preemptive strike and missed the Italian restaurant where they launder money. Weeds worked hard to survive. The guilt bush needed a trim, and extenuating circumstance had gotten out of hand. Apologies had been planted, with a compromise and several retreats. Bookies hid in the fatigue. He missed the point of Trotsky.

Nevertheless, he unbolted the door to the garden. He positioned a chair on the rotting beams of the sun deck. He opened a book full of sinewy prose and shining intelligence. He thought about gin and Budapest. The discrepancies needed watering, and the syllogisms wanted manure, and the broken glass seemed the eyes of cats, marbles veined with useless instinct, menacing piffle. He had hours to form an opinion.

Listen, he said to himself: I haven't done anything dishonorable in at least a week.

And then he whispered: Guess what? I'm *happy*.

Not so loud, said Schopenhauer, not so loud. *They might find out.*

Questions and Answers

We ended up the evening arguing. This usually happens. It happens because she is fiercely intelligent and there are matters, not all of them trivial, on which we disagree. It also happens because she is fiercely beautiful—"beauty like a tightened bow," said Yeats, who then added: "Was there another Troy for her to burn?" —and arguing with her is a way of flirting, a form of courtly love. I cannot, really, bring her a rose in my teeth, or wag my tail, and so instead I shake my head and quibble.

I suspect her husband is aware of what I'm doing, of this pitiful device for engaging her attention. Sitting there behind his beard, he is a pasha of awareness. But I can't help myself.

We were in the kitchen. It is amazing how serious kitchens are. In my experience, kitchens are much more serious than living rooms. In living rooms, we talk about money and weather. In kitchens, we talk about children and history. Maybe kitchens are serious because they are places of fire and water, without television sets. Maybe we are serious in kitchens because we are armed with tools for stabbing and stirring. Anyway, a kitchen seems to be a sort of garage for the emotions, a repair shop. I have, in kitchens, permitted myself to pretend to be profound. It is in bedrooms that I am laughable.

And it had been a good evening. There are evenings in New York to which taximeters are attached; the minutes tick away; we are going into psychic debt; we will never arrive. This had not been one of those evenings. It had been more like Frisbee. Still, there I was in the kitchen, full of fire and water, arguing with Maud Gonne.

About what? About questions. And about answering questions. And about answering questions *with* questions. You will remember the routine. Question: Why do Irishmen always answer a question with another question? Answer: Do we?

Well, this particular Maud Gonne is a psychiatric social worker, some of which she brings home to her children. Asked a question by one of her children, she is concerned first to find out why that question is being asked. A quick, authoritative answer may miss the point—or be beside it. What children ask may not be what they want to know, or it may mean they think they know more than they do and need merely to clarify the wrong detail. Children are notorious for going into battle against the unknown with tangents instead of arrows in their verbal quivers.

We aren't talking now about questions for which there are automatic answers. Later. No. The stork. Because I said so. Have you done your homework? Or the ever-popular "President John F. Kennedy once explained to us that *life* is unfair."

Nor are we talking about questions for which there are no answers, such as the one a friend of mine was asked by her daughter. Her daughter, pondering the meaning of a popular vulgarism used to describe the act of sexual intercourse, asked my friend: "If *bleeping* is supposed to be something people do when they love each other, why are you always angry when you say it?"

For children, all conversations occur in the kitchen, and we are history.

My Maud Gonne meant a question like this: "Mommy, what's leukemia?" A child who asks such a question is thinking about a lot of other things. If her mother is my favorite psychiatric social worker, she will reply: "Well, where did you hear *that* word?" She will hope that her daughter found it in a book, and she will fear that her daughter heard it in the hall between classes at school, or from a stricken friend. The intelligent parent becomes a kindly detective, not a dictionary.

Even though I argued, I understood. But I would have played the part of a very abridged dictionary at the beginning: "Leukemia is a sort of trouble in your blood." No more than that. I've learned the stupidity of elaboration, of speechifying. When my son asks me for his allowance, I no longer explain the theory of surplus value, with digressions on Felix Rohatyn. When my daughter wants to go to the movies, I suppress my Siegfried Kracauer. They'll let me know if they want more than a weather report.

Then, of course, one zeros in. Why, who, what, where, when, how?

Maud Gonne's bearded husband emerged from his trance of awareness long enough to observe that we were arguing about tactics, not principles. As usual, he was right. Or: she was a principle, and I was a tactic. I wasn't even a strategy. Nevertheless.

Nevertheless, I've watched too much Frosting of Nixon, and read too many transcripts. The preeminent literary form of our time may be the transcript of a police interrogation. To reply to a question with a question is to deflect the intelligence. Evasion is our style. What do you want to know, and when did you want to know it? Why do you ask?

Questions, said Wallace Stevens, are remarks. Who, asked Allen Ginsberg, killed the pork chops?

My own wife has at length acquainted me with the advantages of the Socratic method of teaching: we ask our way to what we ought to have known in the first place. My fiercely psychiatric social worker knows fiercely Freud's facsimile of that method: we talk ourselves to hard truths, without shoes on our tongues, in the company of drovers, amiable cops, mystagogues. We are inadvertently significant—in our dreams and jokes, habits and questions.

But Plato and Freud had systems of absolutes going for them. If I were a child, I'd prefer a straight answer. If that answer didn't tell me all I needed to know, I'd ask some more. It's tough enough being dumb and innocent; spare me systematic games. I'd petition my parents for redress of confusion and if they hit me over the head with a Zen or Sufi enigmatic question mark, I'd declare my independence. I don't want to flap, like 'Attār's lapwing, across the Seven Valleys of Mystical Experience to Annihilation of the Self, and ask, "What does it mean?" only to be told, "Who wants to know?" or, "What's it to you?" Not in my Troy or kitchen.

The Sweet Science

In a lifetime of excess and inadvertence, of guile and autodidacticism, I have given up a number of things. In no particular order of importance, I have given up dessert, croquet, Thomas Wolfe, three-piece suits, political ambitions, secretaries, owning a car, singing "Danny Boy," the Ptolemaic system of astronomy, the dream of the Enlightenment, several inconvenient scruples, Sophia Loren, Lent and cigarettes (six times).

I regret Sophia Loren.

So far as I can tell, the cosmos has been untroubled by those manful relinquishings. If, as Eddington once suggested, life itself is merely the messy consequence of "a lack of antiseptic precautions on the part of the cosmos," no wonder. If the cosmos couldn't be bothered to worry about its personal hygiene, it isn't going to worry about me. And the news that I have now given up boxing isn't going to punch any black holes in its cold harmony.

It happened two weeks ago. I was down in the dungeon watching television and feeding myself, as though I were Darwin's insectivorous sundew flower, with bits of cork and stone, snake poison and tissue from the visceral cavity of a toad. On television was what they purported to be a heavyweight championship prizefight between Muhammad Ali and Alfredo Evangelista.

I am not easily bored. I have been to Cleveland, and finished the diaries of Anaïs Nin.

But even Howard Cosell was bored. (I will say no more about Howard Cosell; as subject or object, Howard Cosell is another one of the things I have given up.) Ali—well, Ali gets in the way. Better minds than mine have dilated on the phenomenon of his celebrityhood, in articles and books commissioned by editors for whom he is the Jacqueline Onassis of the sweat set. James Baldwin, Wilfrid Sheed and Garry Wills had a go. Norman Mailer, George Plimpton, Hunter S. Thompson and Budd Schulberg went off to the ex-Congo for the Foreman fight, took Drew "Bundini" Brown as seriously as Robert or the other Moses, and composed monographs on rope-a-dope.

Many articles have been written on why Ali, suddenly, is no longer interesting. This is not one of them.

Boredom, it seems to me, is a signal, an alarm. It means more than itself. Just as a fever is the body's way of saying we're full of internal contradictions—we aren't sick because of the fever; the fever is explaining that we're sick for some other reason—so boredom is ringing a bell on a sort of psychic thermostat or smoke detector. The brain's in trouble, and the trouble isn't boredom. We can shop around for another distraction, or we can think about what's wrong.

That Ali *was* so interesting for so long kept us from thinking about what's wrong. What's wrong is boxing, which is less a "sweet science" than it is a racket consisting for the most part of thugs manipulating morons. If the morons weren't moronic to begin with, more often than not they'll end up that way, after the pounding. For every Ali, there are two hundred cauliflower heads, and millions of stay-at-home morons watching it happen on television.

Yeah, I rooted for Sugar Ray Leonard at the Montreal Olympics. The reason should be obvious. I hope he doesn't end up like Joe Louis. And several years ago, on the occasion of the first Ali-Frazier fight, I accepted a ticket to Madison Square Garden. Four of us went to dinner before that fight. Our host, for dinner and fight, was eventually to publish Ali's autobiography. His guests were the editor of an influential book-reviewing magazine, the head of a major paperback publishing company and a vice-president of an important book club. My guess is that none of us had thrown a punch since high school.

Men get excited at prizefights. Men also get excited reading newspaper accounts of rape. Men tend to be sick.

Of course, prizefighting is a means of upward mobility, like the church, the army, trade unionism and organized crime. You don't see a Lowell or a Cabot in the ring. Variously, according to the dispensation of whoever uses the Social Contract to blow his aquiline nose with, you see the Irish and the Italians and the blacks and the Puerto Ricans trying to kill one another in the name of sport. If boxing is the only way out of poverty and discrimination, maybe we should change the society that determines the options.

And of course an artful few will review a prizefight as if it were ballet. Everywhere you look, aesthetics: note the choreography of the rape scenes in *A Clockwork Orange* and *Death Wish*. The fan wants blood. The fan wears a Benny "Kid" Paret T-shirt. We are talking about the brain, a tangle of synapses in a bowl of bone, a kind of cathedral at Chartres made out of flesh and electricity at which evolution has been agonizing for millions of years. We would bomb it.

There are sports in the prosecution of which we break arms, legs and collarbones instead of brains.

And cockfights are illegal in this imperial city.

Watching Ali and Evangelista, I realized that I was bored because I wanted Ali to take out this stiff by the fifth round. Enough of the shuffle and the rope-a-dope. Be our hero; dance on his head, sweet fists; sting with greatness. Ali is too old and therefore boring.

What fun. I recant. This account, then, is liable to an interpretation of conflicted namby-pambyism. Once upon a time, in gym class, they tried to make a man of me, but this morning I am ambivalent.

Although I keep trying, one of the things I haven't quite been able to give up yet is feeling ashamed of myself.

My Son, the Roman

In a month or so, he will be fifteen, which is absurd. I never intended him to be old enough to contemplate driving a car or applying to college. He was supposed to stay eight, or maybe twelve. I examine him for stigmata of sullenness; no, merely the clouded look of afternoons with books, and, where the light collects—at the rims of his aviator glasses, in the braces on his teeth —some fire. His feet are huge; I have ordered seven-league boots.

According to a Hungarian proverb, the owl always believes his son is a hawk.

He is reporting on the folkways of inscrutable Florida. It seems that the students of Latin are restless. All over Florida the students of Latin in junior and senior high schools have been agitating. Each school competes against the other schools in each city. Winners then advance to a state competition in Miami. There will be a national competition later this summer.

What do they compete about? He explains: Roman history, Roman literature, Latin grammar and vocabulary, costumes. They build chariots and stage skits. I quote Heinrich Heine: "The Romans would never have found time to conquer the world if they had been obliged first to learn Latin." But Latin is his favorite subject. I tell him that the Greeks built the Parthenon and the Romans built sewers. But he is checking up on Claudius in Robert Graves.

The idea that everybody in Florida is learning Latin for some reason makes me uneasy. Is it a language in which peninsulas specialize?

He describes at length his trip to Miami for the state competition. He doesn't much approve of Miami as a town. But they spent the night in a hotel, and they stayed up late, well past their curfew, and they played poker for real money. He is excited: he won seventy-five cents. What's more—and he lowers his voice, as if Tiberius might be listening—they drank beer.

His father, who once kept Anheuser-Busch in business, wants to know how much beer they drank at night in a hotel room in Miami. A can, says his son. A can apiece? No, a can period. An eighteen-year-old girl bought a sixteen-ounce can of beer and they all had sips while playing poker for real money after curfew. And on the bus ride back from Miami they sang songs, making up verses that poked fun at Roman history.

Remember when sin was fun? I once said in this space that not only wouldn't I want to be sixteen years old again, but that I hadn't wanted to be sixteen years old the first time. Other people, however, are entitled. Now if only it were possible to skip the terrors of sexuality, to buy nostalgia like a golden oldie without having gone through the bruising experience. Authenticity is overrated.

He has more to report. At the end of the school year, the Latin classes have a banquet. The week before the banquet there is an auction. At this auction the advanced students, those in Latin II and Latin III, bid on members of the Latin I class and buy them as slaves. The money spent at the auction helps pay for the banquet. A slave, if he is caught by his master, is obliged to carry books, fetch sodas, walk to class on his knees, run around the quad at lunchtime shouting, "The British are coming" and otherwise make a fool of himself.

I approve of slavery as a pedagogical device somewhat less than my son approves of Miami. But of course it's very Roman, like so many quaint customs that have come down from the Empire to modern statecraft. (Whereas Caesar wouldn't even read Pompey's mail, Tiberius specialized in paid informers and considered almost anything that annoyed him to be high treason.) And the slaves were freed at midnight after the banquet.

This freedom allowed them, the following weekend, to go to the Latin beach party. The beach party marks the end of the busy social season for students of Latin in a Florida public high school. By car caravan, they seek the sea and sand. The cars, I am told, all had CB radios, and the students of Latin monopolized a channel. At the beach they ate and drank and swam and ate and drank. They also gathered for one last rendition of the number in their skit that brought down the house in Miami.

In this number, hooded figures come on stage and lurk. They are ordered to identify themselves. They remove their hoods, are revealed to be wearing sunglasses, and, to the tune of a popular rock approximation of music, burst into song:

> *Ba-ba-ba*
> *Bar-bar-a-barians*
> *Ba-ba-ba*
> *Bar-bar-a-barians . . .*

And so on.

I am unglued. Fatherhood flounders. A wheel fell off my Oedipal cycle. Yes, it's true: when the barbarians arrive, it will be in snowmobiles with CB radios. My son will be reading Lucretius, or playing the clarinet while condominiums burn. I will go for beer. "No poems can please for long or live that were written by water-drinkers," said Horace in a hot epistle.

In my youth, in the jumbo-shrimp shacks and taco parlors along the southern California coast, the surfers couldn't speak English, much less Latin. I never went to a beach party where I wasn't humiliated. Grunion always ran the other way. I flunked volleyball and puberty rite. Can it be that my son is going to be happier being young than I was? If so, and even though he deserves it, poker-faced behind my sunglasses, I will never let him know. It would be bad for his character.

Crazy in the Kitchen

As is usually not the case, Dmitri's friend was serious. "I feel like a Russian novel," he said. And he looked like one, too, intellectually disheveled, as though he had been wandering around in the rain for years in search of somebody to whom he could explain himself, as though there were birds and stones in his pockets.

In fact, there was a letter.

Their friendship was typical of men in New York. It was a kind of cuffing, a verbal scuffle. They complained about their work, and tried to improve on each other's jokes, and were generally hard on the world. Their affection wore boxing gloves. It is against the rules of New York manhood to *need* a friend, or at least a male friend. When you are pounced on by emotions, you go to women.

And so when his friend called and said he needed to talk, Dmitri was at a loss. First of all, he didn't want to hear that his friend had lost his job, or that his marriage was falling apart. News of this sort no longer surprised Dmitri, but neither did it leave him much to say. It caused a sad blankness; you wanted to put your thumbs in your eyes. Words were as heavy as medicine balls, and you dropped them.

Secondly, where would they talk? Women took their trouble into the kitchen and made coffee. While waiting for the coffee, they began to talk, and by the time the coffee was ready, they were in the middle of it; coffee was a form of punctuation, or the turning of a page. Whereas men stood around wondering what to do with their hands, and then fixed drinks, and then stood around sipping their drinks, and finally sat down in the living room because there was no point in standing up, and, having solved the problem of what to do with their hands, faced the problem of what to do with their feet, whether or not to cross their legs, how to begin, in what kind of crouch appropriate to their seriousness. Men began cold, having already used up their punctuation. It was, really, as if they lacked a grammar for the emotions.

Dmitri compromised by fixing drinks in the kitchen. That way, they could immediately sit down at the round oak table, with a place for their elbows, hiding their feet.

His friend told him about feeling like a Russian novel and handed him the letter. "Read it, please."

Dmitri did as he was told. It was handwritten. The first page inquired into the whereabouts of someone named Max. Was Max dead, or had the correspondent been misinformed? If he had been misinformed, was it deliberate? The next three pages asked whether Dmitri's friend would be willing to collaborate with the correspondent on a science-fiction novel exposing "the *real* nature" of Christianity.

Now that we have seen that space travel is possible, the letter went on, it seems obvious that higher intelligences from other star systems have been traveling in space for thousands of years. In the letter writer's opinion, John the Baptist was sent as an emissary from an advanced civilization to earth to prepare us for the coming of Christ. The Virgin Birth was explained by artificial insemination. And so on.

Dmitri put the letter on the table. "What do you think?" asked his friend.

"Who is Max?"

"My younger brother." Dmitri hadn't known his friend had a brother. "In a way, I'm not sure I do anymore," said his friend, "but what about the rest of it? John the Baptist?"

"He's crazy," said Dmitri. "Who is he?"

His friend, in silence, seemed to be consulting some inner compass to see which way it pointed. He punctuated: he sipped his drink. "My stepfather," he said at last. "The only person in the world I hate."

Dmitri's friend had often joked that he had attended three of his mother's weddings, missing only the first one. Beyond that, details had not been forthcoming. They came now, of the Kirk Douglas look-alike who had entered his life when he was eleven and his brother seven; whose dimples had followed his mother across the country until she agreed to marriage; who set up shop as a breakfast-table sadist and stayed in business for the next twelve years; who would make men out of boys.

Making men out of boys meant teaching them to bowl, and to wash his car, and to play cards, and to stand up to all bullies except the one in their own home. It meant taking them to barns to catch pigeons in sacks, then cutting the throats of the pigeons and plucking out their feathers in the garage. It meant week-long rages, three-day sulks and other women. It meant not bringing your friends home so they wouldn't see your mother get slapped around. It meant going to school with fingerprints on your face and arms.

Dmitri's friend was old enough to duck and quick enough to hide, through high school and into college. His younger brother had to stick it out all twelve years, and when he finally escaped to college, it was to find the other side of the moon in drugs and to come home with a broken brain. Max disappears for years at a time. Then the police find him.

Dmitri's friend hadn't heard from his stepfather in more than fifteen years. His mother, now happily remarried, hadn't heard from him in ten. "And now, three thousand miles away, he sends me this letter. And you say he's crazy." They had been in the kitchen for a couple of hours and as much Scotch. "You know, I've never been in analysis or therapy." Neither had Dmitri; it was one of their odd ties, like their profound suspicion of astrology and vegetarianism. Where was the music?

"And I was right," said his friend. "*I'm* not crazy. *He's* crazy. I don't have to work it out. I hate him, and I damn well should. It was nice of him, don't you think, to write me a crazy letter. *Proof!* The secret is out! John the Baptist!" He looked around the kitchen. "Now, if only I had Salome and a plate."

Dmitri knew that his friend wanted to cry, but wouldn't in front of a man.

Red Rover

Soon we leave, in one of those tin pterodactyls that abolish the decency of distance between the East Coast and the West. I shall have to cope with the terrors of leisure for a month. In the mountains, overgrown with children, lacking any work to hide behind, I am opposed by the fidgets. A couple of years ago was the summer of the rattlesnake. I had thought at first to vanquish the rattlesnake with an acetylene torch, which would have been a good way to set all of drought-ridden southern California on fire. I settled instead for a shovel, and that was fine; it gave us something to talk about.

Not for the first time, it occurs to me that writing about private life is an excellent excuse for not having one.

Anyway, knowing we were soon to leave lent a valedictory quality to last Saturday's shenanigans, a sort of autumnal rot of the emotions in mid-June. Last Saturday was also like a practice run, as if, before we could go to California, we had to go to New Jersey, and so we went to New Jersey. I know it was dangerous; it is always dangerous to leave the imperial city. That is why they let you go to New Jersey for free, but you have to pay to come back.

There, in New Jersey, I sat, in an extra pair of tennis sneakers borrowed from my son, the Latin Scholar. His tennis sneakers were too big for me. If any remarks are to be made about stepping into your son's shoes, I will make them, and I'd rather not. The sun fell down on the other side of the reservoir. The lawn was littered with the bodies of little children.

We had spent the afternoon playing slow-pitch softball in a public park inexplicably bereft of other bipeds. It turned out to be more fun than killing rattlesnakes. Adult males had to bat one-handed, and no balls or strikes were called; you stayed at the plate until you hit something. In two games, there were only three failures of character, two temper tantrums, one pair of broken glasses and one missing child (out of a consignment of eleven).

Time then, having proved we were regular fellows—and while the children persisted maniacally at basketball and volleyball and tag—to relax in the vicinity of cold beer and to contemplate the altar of the outdoor grill upon which cows and pigs were sacrificed. I am forever told to relax, as though the goal of the human experiment were an integral sloth. I prefer, instead, to sublimate, and to practice my Hegelianism, which seeks its Self in its Other, the "other," of course, being experienced as a harsh purification of the "self," like hitting into a double play.

And, looking warily around at the company of adults in which I had chosen to practice my Hegelianism, I thought they were probably sublimating, too. What, after all, was the point of the neocortex, if not to transcend our compost heap of instincts? Like me, many of these adults were scribblers. Among us we must have perpetrated five million words in the last five years. Although the world had been in no way altered by those millions of words—we must live together and die alone—Monday morning would find us once more tethered to our typewriters with our tragic sense of the discrepancies.

We consumed our ritual sacrifice. We slandered our employers. I thought of fetching another beer, but deferred the gratification. And as the children, armed with plastic cups, declared war on fireflies, we waxed metaphysical. "Life in the suburbs," said one of the scribblers, "is more spontaneous."

I took this seriously. I take everything seriously. According to T. S. Eliot, "In the mountains, there you feel free." Now I was being told: "In the suburbs, there you feel spontaneous." I reminded myself that only a vulgarian is certain of first principles. Nevertheless, can any way of life that depends on the existence of station wagons be considered truly spontaneous?

Besides, when anybody criticizes, even by implication, the imperial city, I take umbrage and the two of us go to a delicatessen. New York may be one big crystallized superego; it is certainly a pile of guilt. Guilt, however, has its sweet uses. It is a source of energy and a gauge of consciousness. Living in the suburbs has always seemed to me like dramatizing *Oedipus Rex* in front of an audience of Peter Pans. However agreeable the Peter Pans, they miss the point. The suburbs are a Veil of Maya; New York is a Bindu Dot.

"Don't you agree," I was asked, "that life in the suburbs is more spontaneous?" I am nothing if not civil. "I have eaten," I told them, "too many Heisenbergers, and the uncertainty is killing me." Somewhere inside the house, there was a beer with my number on it. Maybe I would place a telephone call to Woody Allen: Let's draft a petition in favor of neurosis.

Hard to believe, but the children were now playing Red Rover. By the cold light of fireflies, they linked hands in two opposing lines. One team would summon a child from the line of the other team. That child was then obliged to hurl himself or herself at the opposing team and try to snap a link. At one portentous moment, five big girls faced off against five little boys, and a little boy was heard to say: "We are in trouble." They played, unto concussion, for hours.

We moved the lawn furniture so as to watch, the moon doing the best it could for dangerous New Jersey, where they use mobsters as fertilizer. "It's better than the Super Bowl," said another scribbler. He was right. Maybe California and the mountains would be better than the Super Bowl, too. I thought about leisure, and about how I would devote my leisure to considering the nature of work, and my various anaclitic hang-ups, and why it was, even though I had grown up in the suburbs, I had never as a child played Red Rover, and yet I will spend the rest of my adult spontaneity playing a game that seems almost exactly like it.

The Only Child

He is big. He always has been, over six feet, with that slump of the shoulders and tuck in the neck big men in this country often affect, as if to apologize for being above the democratic norm in size. (In high school and at college he played varsity basketball. In high school he was senior class president.) And he looks healthy enough, blue-eyed behind his beard, like a trapper or a mountain man, acquainted with silences. He also grins a lot.

Odd, then, to have noticed earlier—at the house, when he took off his shabby coat to play Ping-Pong—that the white arms were unmuscled. The coat may have been a comment. This, after all, is southern California, where every man is an artist, an advertiser of himself; where every surface is painted and every object potted; where even the statues seem to wear socks. The entire population ambles, in polyesters, toward a Taco Bell. To wear a brown shabby cloth coat in southern California is to admit something.

So he hasn't been getting much exercise. Nor would the children have elected him president of any class. At the house they avoided him. Or, since he was too big to be avoided entirely, they treated his presence as a kind of odor to pass through hurriedly, to be safe on the other side. They behaved like cats. Of course, he ignored them. But I think they were up to more than just protecting themselves from his lack of curiosity. Children are expert readers of grins.

His grin is intermittent. The dimples twitch on and off; between them, teeth are bared; above them, the blue eyes disappear in a wince. This grin isn't connected to any humor the children know about. It may be a tic. It could also be a function of some metronome made on Mars. It registers inappropriate intervals. We aren't listening to the same music.

This is the man who introduced me to the mysteries of

mathematical science, the man I could never beat at chess, the man who wrote haiku and played with computers. Now there is static in his head, as though the mind had drifted off its signal during sleep. He has an attention span of about thirty seconds.

I am to take him back to where he lives, in the car I have rented in order to pretend to be a Californian. We are headed for a rooming house in one of the beach cities along a coast of off-ramps and oil wells. It is a rooming house that thinks of itself as Spanish. The ruined-hacienda look requires a patio, a palm tree and several miles of corrugated tile. He does not expect me to come up to his room, but I insist. I have brought along a six-pack of beer.

The room is a slum, and it stinks. It is wall-to-wall beer cans, hundreds of them, under a film of ash. He lights cigarettes and leaves them burning on the windowsill or the edge of the dresser or the lip of the sink, while he thinks of something else—Gupta sculpture, maybe, or the Sephiroth Tree of the Kabbalah. The sink is filthy, and so is the toilet. Holes have been burnt in the sheet on the bed, where he sits. He likes to crush the beer cans after he has emptied them, then toss them aside.

He tells me that he is making a statement, that this room is a statement, that the landlord will understand the meaning of his statement. In a week or so, according to the pattern, they will evict him, and someone will find him another room, which he will turn into another statement, with the help of the welfare checks he receives on account of his disability, which is the static in his head.

There are no books, no newspapers or magazines, no pictures on the wall. There is a television set, which he watches all day long while drinking beer and smoking cigarettes. I am sufficiently familiar with the literature on schizophrenia to realize that this room is a statement he is making about himself. I am also sufficiently familiar with his history to understand that, along with his contempt for himself, there is an abiding arrogance. He refuses medication. They can't make him take it, any more than they can keep him in a hospital. He has harmed no one. One night, in one of these rooms, he will set himself on fire.

He talks. Or blurts: scraps from Oriental philosophers—
Lao-tzu, I think—puns, incantations, obscenities, names from the
past. There are conspiracies; I am part of one of them. He grins,
winces, slumps, is suddenly tired, wants me to get out almost as
much as I want to get out, seems to have lapsed in a permanent
parenthesis. Anyway, I have a busy schedule.

Well, speed kills slowly, and he fiddled too much with the
oxygen flow to his brain. He wanted ecstasy and revelation, the
way we grew up wanting a bicycle, a car, a girlfriend. These belonged to us by right, as middle-class Americans. So, then, did
salvation belong to us by right. I would like to thank Timothy
Leary and all the other sports of the 1960's who helped make this
bad trip possible. I wish R. D. Laing would explain to me, once
again and slowly, how madness is a proof of grace. "The greatest
magician," said Novalis, "would be the one who would cast over
himself a spell so complete that he would take his own phantas-
magorias as autonomous appearances."

One goes back to the rented car and pretending to be a
Californian as, perhaps, one had been pretending to be a brother.
It is odd, at my age, suddenly to have become an only child.

When Naiads Meet Raccoons

Dmitri sits on the sun deck of the mountain cabin, listening to his skin peel. He does not tan; he rots. The sun deck looks down on a creek. Bravely, the creek keeps on trickling, although it seems not to have rained in these mountains since Nixon went to China. They have tried to dam the creek. Why, Dmitri's son was asked, are you building a dam? "Because it isn't there," Dmitri's son replied. Dmitri's son has hired some new writers for the summer.

In fact, they are damming the creek to make a water hole to swim in. This has been a project undertaken every summer, hitherto without success. The hole fills up with sand and gravel faster than Dmitri's son can shovel it out. This summer, however, they engaged the services of a three-inch pump, and, after a death-defying descent into the ravine, used the pump like a monstrous vacuum cleaner to tame the brave waters of the creek. Thus: three feet of hole.

And, possibly, pneumonia. Creeks in the mountains are cold. The whole family stood for days in the creek with shovels, first turning blue and then transparent. From the deck, one could have seen their arterial systems. If they had been drinking wine, they would have looked like upside-down thermometers.

It is still not enough hole for Dmitri's son to swim in. By next summer, he will be too big for the ravine. But he stands watch, on a hot rock, as his sisters swim and Dmitri thinks about naiads. He would prefer, on the whole, to think about naiads than to think about blue jays. Blue jays are overrated. They have nasty expressions and are mean to squirrels. Consider, on the other hand, the hummingbird, who minds his own business and is content with a bottle of colored water. It is clear that the idea of the helicopter originated with the hummingbird; helicopters are big noisy hummingbirds who mind other people's business, like blue jays. The idea of the White House Plumbers originated with blue jays.

Maybe Dmitri should bring the three-inch pump up on the sun deck and vacuum the blue jays.

We will think about the raccoons later on.

The naiads want to play Monopoly. When they aren't swimming, or listening to the radio, or eating cherries and peanut butter, or reading *The Doonesbury Chronicles*, they play Monopoly or Parcheesi or backgammon, and slam doors. That is the way the day goes, except for a trip into town. Arrowbear doesn't count as a town because you can't buy a newspaper in Arrowbear. Someone in Arrowbear put up a sign saying ARROWBEAR LOVES YOU, and the fire inspector took it down for fear it would attract hippies and other perverts. So a trip to town is a trip to Running Springs, by car.

This means that every morning Dmitri is deprived of his information-fix. He sits on the sun deck surrounded by fine prose—new books by Paul Scott, Toni Morrison, Don DeLillo and Jonathan Yardley—but not knowing what the Dodgers or the C.I.A. did yesterday. He could consult the radio. He does not because the cabin receives only one station, a Top 40 ear sore, and he will not allow the radio to be turned on until four o'clock in the afternoon, when he goes to town.

The naiads want to know what he thinks of Stevie Wonder. Outasight, said Dmitri. This is a good way to lose the respect of your children. Deservedly. Dmitri punishes himself by playing Monopoly, a game he likes almost as much as he likes blue jays.

Raccoons, though, inspire a certain respect. For one thing, they won't eat beets. The raccoons show up at the cabin every night around eleven o'clock, which is approximately bedtime for the children. From four o'clock until dinner the children have been gorging themselves on the Top 40. On the occasion of the first mosquito, Dmitri suggests to his son that a fire be ignited in the barbecue rotisserie. Dmitri then burns meat, feeling for the first time in his life that he is an authentic American male. This meat consumed, and the dishes cleared away, the family sits down to play word games: Botticelli, Dictionary or Categories. When Dmitri loses, they check out the raccoons.

They are a pair, the raccoons, and specialize in knocking over garbage cans. What remains of dinner is left out for them. Everything disappears except beets. When they become aware that the family has gathered to watch them, they climb up an embankment behind the kitchen window and watch the family. Dmitri wonders if a raccoon knows that he is cute. Is cuteness a raccoon category?

Dmitri also remembers the story of a friend who watched a raccoon steal away with a box of graham crackers. The raccoon opened the package, took out a cracker, and carefully washed it in a stream. The cracker, naturally, disintegrated. No more cracker. Then on to the next. And the next. And the one after that. A whole box of graham crackers, gone. Maybe instinct is overrated.

Certainly television is, and perhaps the typewriter. Dmitri has promised his children not to touch a typewriter for a month, and they are without a television set, and his son reads Roman history and his wife reads *War and Peace* and everybody plays Botticelli, and when dawn comes up like a sword over a swimming hole full of trout he counts the heads of his family and for once it all adds up and he dares—having vacated, his skin falling off, low on gin, Arrowbear loves you—to entertain the proposition that being a father, really, isn't such hard work. Fixed with that information, he amazes himself by relaxing.

Father Bird

We went to Fire Island in the middle of the week, in the middle of a monsoon, to hole up at a friend's house because the city was too much. The idea was, I suppose, to pull the self over one's head, like a poncho, and hide inside it until the bloodstorm stopped.

I may have gotten the idea when I saw people on the street selling "Son of Sam" T-shirts, complete with the police sketch, the police telephone number and the slogan GET HIM BEFORE HE GETS YOU. Capitalism strikes again.

I no longer wanted to think about Jimmy Breslin or Abe Beame.

Then, of course, there were the events on our block. During our first week back from California, the police lived on our block. They closed down the local after-hours gambling casino again. They probably didn't want to, but a man with a broken leg had been locked inside the casino overnight and couldn't get out and screamed for help, and after the police broke down several sets of doors they found the liquor and dice and cards and so on. So a third raid in as many months was necessary, along with a lot of paperwork.

The dressmaker who worked two doors down and had been missing for a couple of days was found dead in her furnished room.

In the apartment house next door, in the middle of the afternoon, somebody jumped out of a window into the concrete courtyard. The police and an ambulance arrived within minutes. Within an hour, the superintendent of the apartment house was scrubbing down the concrete with Clorox.

The following day the police were slower to arrive, and an ambulance refused to come at all. A young boy, maybe nineteen, was behaving oddly, lurching about, staggering into traffic, hanging onto lampposts. It could have been a fit of some sort. More likely it was drugs. Clearly, he was a danger to himself, although the people in the Mexican restaurant on the corner were more worried about their plate-glass window. Better he should fall down in the street.

We tried to sit him down. He was incoherent. We walked with him. He smashed into people. Authorities were telephoned. Lenox Hill Hospital would not dispatch an ambulance unless the boy himself requested it, and he wasn't even requesting directions. After fifteen minutes, the police came: What was he on? Where did he live? Where was he going? He didn't know, or wasn't telling. They shrugged. What were they supposed to do with him? What they did was move him on. Get a bus, they said to him. To us, they said, "It's his own fault." He stumbled, and they drove away.

This is the way the world works. If you have a broken leg and scream for help, or if you are found dead in your room, or if you jump out of a window, you are an event, an occasion, and you will be dealt with. If you have a broken mind, have fallen out of reality, can't ask for help, keep moving, catch a bus, it's your own fault. When he gets hit by a car, they will take him to the hospital because then he will have authenticated himself.

I should explain that our block is in Yorkville. I point this out because a while ago there was an article in *Commonweal* magazine by Peter Steinfels about the white liberal failure of nerve, the fatigue of idealism Mr. Steinfels perceived in our dealings in this city with the disadvantaged black and Hispanic minorities. I am nothing if not a white liberal. Wishy-washy is my middle name. So naturally I agreed with much of Mr. Steinfels's article. We ought not give up trying to reupholster the commonwealth more equably. Our mission is to feel bad.

Nevertheless, I was perplexed to find that one of my own columns—the one on the slobs who used to mess up my stoop—was cited as evidence of this liberal fatigue. I was also perplexed to hear that my stoop was on the West Side. I went on reading about the unemployment figures for the minority young. All right, those figures are disgraceful, but what had they to do with my column? What had I done *this* time? I live on the East Side, and the slobs who messed up my stoop were white, middle-class kids who go to the same junior high school my son went to.

I no longer want to think about Jimmy Breslin, Abe Beame or liberals who assume that when one writes about slobs on a stoop, one must be writing about black or Hispanic slobs on a West Side stoop. Such an assumption might even be illiberal.

So we went to liberal Fire Island, which is even whiter than my stoop. Nobody dies, or jumps out of windows on Fire Island, although I am told the police run over nude sunbathers because they can't see them in the sand. And I met the bird.

Who knows what kind of bird? A father bird. Mother bird was in the bushes with a platoon of birdlets. Father bird screamed all day long, as though he were locked up in a gambling casino. He was screaming at a ten-year-old cat so arthritic that she could barely switch her tail. Should the cat appear at a window or try to find a spot of shade under a deck chair, father bird would scream and dive-bomb. It wasn't safe on the white, liberal porch.

At first I was impressed at father bird's devotion to his birdlets: he would terrorize the fierce, immobile cat. Then I felt maybe he was protesting too much, as is the nature of fathers. Finally I concluded he was a pain in the poncho, either stupid or having nothing better to do than keep me from thinking about Breslin, Beame and the sociology of stoops. Squirting the hose at him to shut his beak seemed a better idea than Fire Island or a "Son of Sam" T-shirt. How would Hemingway have handled it? Hemingway would have handled it by saying, It is good to squirt the bird.

Wrong again. The cat was liberal fatigue, on white Fire Island. The bird was a telephone, a headline, an all-news radio bulletin, an alarm clock. The hose was prose, a deflection from self. In Yorkville, they were jumping out of windows, and someone ought to be there to catch them, instead of buses or ferries. The city to which I belonged was too much, which is why I belonged there. Late is my tense.

Rainbowed

The city was behaving itself, as one hopes it will when a young woman is being shown around. The young woman had lived all of her eighteen years in the boondocks. The city owed her something —bagels, anecdotes, verticality, a zap to the synaptic cleft. With perfect composure, she rode a subway. Bloomingdale's did whatever Bloomingdale's does. So did the Village, that boutique of the counterculture. If, at a Mexican restaurant, the guitars were demented, at least there were no accordions. She was stunned by *For Colored Girls Who Have Considered Suicide When the Rainbow Is Enuf*. Had she not been, we would have mailed her home.

I expanded. My city, showing off. Even the freaks on Broadway had hired a choreographer: *entrechat six*, super-strut. Why not, then, a nightcap in one of the caves in one of the mountains in midtown, with wraparound skyline? If Rockefeller Center had a heart, it was probably the RCA Building, which was within walking distance and on top of which—ah, symmetry!—was the Rainbow Room. Through such a periscope, we might see Brooklyn.

The Rainbow Room was not enuf. Or I was not enuf for the Rainbow Room. The Rainbow Room wouldn't let me in. Now I was neat, but not gaudy. I wore shoes and the better class of credit cards. It was my jacket they objected to. They said it wasn't a jacket, and gentlemen were not allowed in the Rainbow Room without a jacket.

I looked at what I had always thought of as a jacket. It is forest green, herringbone weave, pure cotton, made in Ireland, a gift from the woman in my life, and cost twice as much as my shoes. It has dignity and one pocket, no bangles, no chains.

Then I looked inside the Rainbow Room. In leisure suits and sandwich boards, black domino and graffiti-speckled culottes, in bandages and umbrellas and barber poles and pimpmobiles—they lolled, as if they had just arrived by parachute from a rock opera with bad vibes. Who says sheared French rabbit is better than Irish cotton? Where is any of this written? How strait is a jacket supposed to be?

Finally, I looked at the face of the man who had decided that my jacket wasn't a jacket. This face looked like an orthopedic boot.

Well, not to fuss. Fussing is square. If the mission of the liberal intelligence in an age of goons is to feel bad, our hobby is probably embarrassment. According to the Rainbow Room, I didn't belong, although my comrades were permissible. I offered to retire and sulk, that my comrades might enjoy the skyline. Loyally, they dogged me to the elevator. Diminishing, I sank; the lobby was shame.

All right, of course. In the history of human disappointment, not getting into the Rainbow Room isn't worth a footnote. Napoleon III, for example, must have felt much worse when Miss Lawrence of Massachusetts turned down his marriage proposal because she was waiting for a Lowell. With me, though, everything is harrowingly personal. So I brooded all the way to the Stanhope.

At the Stanhope's outdoor café, across Fifth Avenue from the Metropolitan Museum of Art, where they hadn't turned on the water for the fountains, I lit up a rank cheroot and brooded at my pisco sour. (Not really. Smoking rank cheroots, or Indonesian cigarettes, is like smoking carcinogenic perfume, or New York. And ever since reading an article about pisco sours sipped in a four-masted barque off the coast of Peru, I fantasize. But I *did* brood.) Would Elvis Presley have gotten into the Rainbow Room? Or Cotton Mather?

Nine years ago, at an elementary public school in this show-off city, there was a dress code. Little boys were made to wear ties and white shirts every day of the week. Lined up, according to size, in the yard each morning, they looked like miniature mobsters spruced down for a court appearance on tax-evasion charges. An hour later, that spruceness would come unsprung. A smudge obtained, along with the stupidity of not allowing little boys to be little.

This code was illegal, as I'm sure the Rainbow Room's Jacobinism would be, should anybody be so square as to sue. For my son, as for me, I favored—neat, but not gaudy—turtlenecks. One of the functions of sons is to sacrifice themselves for their fathers' principles. Each morning my son's principal yanked him out of line, made him wait until the rest of the prisoners were locked up in their cells, and then sent him home with a reprimand.

The liberal me bestirred itself. Letters to the principal having unavailed, I posted my body in the schoolyard. Seeing my son harassed, I intervened. This principal was a tired man, worried about Albert Shanker. My principles were fresh from a microwave oven: I explained democracy, and the rainbow of style, and the economics of haberdashing. He got sad, and *I* felt bad. Both of us, historians of human disappointment, had more important things to brood about. I prevailed, because once every thirty-seven clashes one happens to prevail.

But, all flashback at the Stanhope, I knew my cause consorted with justice. Anybody who wants us to wear uniforms is infantile-Fascistic. A uniform cut or color, or a list of allowable cuts and colors, is a way of numbering and controlling, an arbitrary code of behavior. Each of us is an indivisible—not an interchangeable—*one*. When we are counted, instead of being accounted for or taken into account, we lose our unique shape and place, even unto our multiplications and squarings. We need not agree with sequins in order to defend in our broods the right of anybody to wear them who wants to. Bad taste, even if I were capable of it, is not a crime.

Listen, Rainbow Room: You serve, taking our money; you do not rule, legislating jacket standards according to Mao or J. P. Morgan or Nehru or Fred Astaire or P. T. Barnum or Liberace. Who do you think you are, anyway? The New York Athletic Club or the Gloucester House? I am at last too old to lick orthopedic boots.

About Cats (II)

There are more kittens. Don't ask how. According to the Yiddish apothegm, "Shoulders are from God, and burdens, too." These kittens look like white rats, but it seems unlikely that the black cat would have littered the clothes closet in the front hall with white rats. Why, when there are clothes closets, suitcases, bureau drawers and plastic trash bags, should anyone have bothered to line a maternity box with newspaper and carpet remnants? How cunning of the black cat to have disdained this box in favor of an old rain boot and one's tennis racket. Perhaps the catgut in the tennis racket overwhelmed her with nostalgia, although we have been reliably informed that catgut is actually the dried intestines of a sheep. Still, sheepgut sounds wrong.

We've had more than enough of the wonder of birth in this house, thank you, sitting around on our knees with a pair of scissors and a smirk. The garden is full of neighborhood toms, each insisting on his personal square of acoustic space. From the window, on the flagstone, they look like pieces in a chess game played with Sumerian fertility symbols. I am, frankly, surprised. I didn't think they cared.

It was necessary to remove the mother and her kittens from the hall closet, in the maternity box, to a cabinet under a sink, where they would be safe from bicycles and vacuum cleaners and Con Ed meter readers and the American Museum of Natural History. Mother, of course, was under the delusion that she knew best. Not two hours later she was stuffing them someplace else. Instinct is boring.

And hard work, too, because the place she decided to stash them was on the top shelf of the bedroom closet. She was thus obliged to take each kitten in her mouth, ascend two flights of stairs, jump onto a dresser and then bound three feet straight up in the air before achieving sanctuary. Having deposited one, she went downstairs for another. And a third. It did no good explaining to her that when her still-blind kittens started to squirm, they would fall off the shelf.

At some personal risk, the kittens were removed from the shelf of the bedroom closet and returned to the cabinet under the sink. The bedroom door was shut to discourage further forays. For the next half-hour the black cat, instead of tending to her kittens, hurled herself at the bedroom door, trying to batter it down with her head. In my cell I fumed. Where, in her neural circuitry or her deoxyribonucleic acids, was it written that kittens belong on closet shelves along with my green beret and my zip gun? Would she really repeat the whole stupid charade?

We let her back into the bedroom. She jumped back up on the dresser, flung herself up on the shelf and pawed around. Down again, then, and out of the bedroom and back to her brood. She did not return. What had she wanted? Of course: *cats can't count.* It was no help to her to know that there were three kittens downstairs; she hadn't the vaguest idea how many kittens she had. It was necessary for her to check the closet shelf and make sure no kitten malingered. Her categories were *all* and *nothing*, like go/no-go. How inexpressibly tedious. If we'd hid a kitten or two in a bowling bag in the boiler room, she would never have known. So far as she was concerned, if it wasn't where she left it, it must be where she put it.

Why am I thinking about cats? Why am I writing about cats? Why, if you haven't already given up on me in justifiable disgust and gone on to the shipping news, are you reading about cats? Why aren't we thinking, writing and reading about Planck's constant, or Stockhausen, or Thutmose III? Because I've had too much summer. There is sand in my brainpan. I require solitude, dreamy exile, the ticking of my books like bombs in an empty house. Maybe after Labor Day I will be able to invent myself some more. These fabrications, these toms of thought, require acoustic space as much as cats do, and shelves.

Listen: do you think it's easy having nothing else to write about but cats?

The women around me don't help. They ought to go back to

school to teach and learn. They ought to bring back anecdotes. Leisure frets them; there are loose strings on the guitars of their days. They sleep late, as if to postpone the problem of purpose. They go from room to room, seeking meaning, watering petunias. They plot picnics, and read novels, and wash their hair, and pile up cheese omelets, and look at the kittens. Everybody in this house sighs.

I could have been in Indochina. I could have disembarked from a purple-sailed pirate junk off the Tonkin coast, tramped with boi-dois in palm-fiber helmets across the Meo highlands, through rain forests lit by bamboo torches; lain with congais in the brothels of Hanoi; thrown stones through the windows of the banks; mown down the rubber trees and coffee bushes of the plantations of Terre Rouge. Cantonese spice and roast pig's bladder! The death gong and the wooden rattle!

Or, imagine the blue-throated doves in the palm trees of Algeria; jackals among burning stones; sheep on spits and sap-gorged flies; refuse-eating cats and tchic-tchic players. I might have hacked my way through cork forests, sand dunes, kif addicts, sluglike Mozabite merchants and French paratroopers; lobbed schneiderite bombs over iron grilles around milk bars and tobacco stalls; slit the esophagi of sentries; sniffed brine, pine, virgin oil and soiled flowers; whistled through reed pipes; watched like a lizard. Fried squid! Spiced couscous and black Mitidja grapes! Istiqlal!

I could have made something of myself as a terrorist or a developing country. What a Living Section I might have been. And here I sit on my shelf with my typewriter, waiting for Labor Day, thinking that never ever again will I write about cats. They have done nothing to deserve me.

Perfect Knowledge in Final Things

We were standing around at a party. Every fall I do a lot of standing around at parties, having forgotten over the summer how much I don't care for standing around at parties with my teeth hanging out. Every fall I imagine once again that something wonderful will happen at a party. This is like imagining that the telephone book will prove to be a wonderful novel. Parties and telephone books have their reasons, but wonder lurks elsewhere, sitting down, in small groups, without any shoes on. Still, in the fall, I will go to a party so long as it isn't on a boat. In my experience, parties on boats are bad news because when I want to go home I am in the middle of the Hudson River with a rock band and an assistant professor of mortuary science.

This particular party, last Thursday, on the day when New Yorkers made the first of the three votes that will be necessary to achieve a new Mayor, contained many of my friends, all of whom had voted. Of my friends' politics, what is there to say? We have lost many, many elections. We all grew up together, losing those elections, reading the same newspapers, magazines and books. We tend, as if history were a kind of pollen, to sneeze the same sneeze. We can be counted on to favor the new Panama Canal treaty and to oppose the death penalty. I suppose we are typical New York liberals.

So typical, in fact, that I felt guilty last year when, almost alone among my peer group, I voted for Jimmy Carter in the Presidential primary. It seemed to me that all my life I had been voting for Mo Udall, even when his name was Adlai Stevenson, and I was tired of losing. This of course, is not political thinking; I just wanted to see what it felt like to back a winner. When I promised never to do it again, my friends let me back into their parties.

Anyway, we found out on Thursday night that we had distributed our votes promiscuously among four or five candidates for Mayor. Some power-hungry peer group I belong to. Not that the news was astonishing. For weeks in this imperial city, everybody has been asking everybody else how he or she intends to vote, and the asking was without rancor. We were participating in a perplexity, and were genuinely interested in one another's reasons, hunches, confusions and confessions. Really, maybe, I hope so, but. On such a loom, the more shuttles the better.

It was the same on Thursday night. We announced our contradictory verdicts. We contemplated the meaning, and the peculiarities, of the franchise. We differed, with respect. We were, with our teeth hanging out, quite solemn but unembittered. We retired with dignity—and the odd sort of innocence that having voted confers.

I like my friends. I like the fact that they vote. In my opinion, not voting causes cancer.

According to H. L. Mencken,

Democracy is that system of government under which the people, having 35,717,342 native-born adult whites to choose from, including thousands who are handsome and many who are wise, pick out a Coolidge to be head of the State. It is as if a hungry man, set before a banquet prepared by master cooks and covering a table an acre in area, should turn his back upon the feast and stay his stomach by catching and eating flies.

In my opinion, H. L. Mencken eats crabgrass. I like voting, on anything. I especially like voting at a public school, although I have wished the students in those schools were required to attend on Election Days, just to watch their parents, as we say, exercise the franchise, as though it were a living thing, which I believe it is. I declare, in privacy, my citizenship. Except in Chicago and Texas, the machine is faithful to my commitment. I feel cleaner afterward. It isn't necessary that I saddle a dolphin or spear a lion: I vote, therefore I am.

At our house, we've been known to hold parties on Election Nights. I resent the laminated anchorpeople on the television screen, consulting their computers to predict what I have done in my singing booth, with my Archimedean lever. I want the total count. Projections dehumanize. For once, people are more important than polls or media consultants or writers of editorials. Spare me the hair spray, molars, sample precincts, sermonettes. What are the numbers?—because I am one of them, and in their flexing the body politic exercises itself.

All right: I am not paid to have political opinions. But those opinions, like my emotions, constitute the private life. Behind the curtain in the auditorium of the public school, I define a part of myself, and never more than when I am uncertain, after a campaign that seemed to have been written by Pirandello. Of what does my citizenship consist? What do I affirm or deny? Which I am I that I can live with?

This much of an I am I: the Mayor of New York has no say on whether human beings may be legally killed by the state, and yet the death penalty was an ugly issue in our primary campaign. I do not believe that killing is legal, not to mention moral. Mitigate the circumstances though we might, extenuations of passion or psychosis notwithstanding, when we murder we do not create. When the state murders, it assumes an authority I refuse to cede: the authority of perfect knowledge in final things. What I have tried, perhaps haplessly, to teach my children; what I trust in my disorderly self; what I wish for our peculiar experiment in sentience; why I vote and feel better having done so—all these argue against the taking of life. If anyone dies because we didn't, at the time, have the facts straight, we participate not in a perplexity but in a murder. And we will never have the facts entirely straight.

The death penalty ought not to have been an issue on Thursday. That it was, though, determined my vote. Of all people, it was Whittaker Chambers who wrote that a man might be murdered meaninglessly:

This reality cuts across our mind like a wound whose edges crave to heal, but cannot. Thus, one of the great sins, perhaps *the* great sin, is to say: It will heal; it has healed; there is no wound; there is something more important than this wound. There is nothing more important than this wound.

The Australians in Paris

I have never met an Australian I didn't like. There may be bad Australians, but they avoid me. Two Australians in particular I think of as saints, if saints drink beer. To explain why, I must go back more than a dozen years. Here, edited for television, is the story.

It was the spring that Lyndon Johnson invaded the Dominican Republic, and Europe was overrun by advertising executives. There was, in fact, an international congress of advertising executives congressing in Paris that spring. This congress had decreed a certain number of scholarships—two weeks in Paris and London— for young people in advertising who were not yet executives. In order to qualify for a scholarship, you had to be under thirty and write an essay on how the "media" might help the developing countries.

Strictly speaking, I was not a young person in advertising. I was a young person who worked as a stringer for a public relations agency. But I'd also never been to Paris or London. My boss pretended that I was in advertising, and I sought to dazzle the French judges of the essay contest with some Marshall McLuhan flimflam, and the gods were kind. Waiting for me in a small hotel across the rue from St. Sulpice were a bottle of champagne, a carton of French cigarettes, a map of the Métro system, a *Le Figaro* key fob and the two Australians.

It is fair to say that we caroused. The trouble was that, unlike the Australians and everybody else at the congress, I had no legitimate business being there. That meant no expense account. I had scraped together a hundred dollars, and almost a third of that had gone for an unhappy taxi ride in from the airport. Still, one picks up a check, one buys a round or one is a creep. Although the Australians grabbed more than their fair share of checks, although the round seemed always to be on them, by the end of the week, with a week yet to come in London, I was down to centimes.

This is the way the week ended. The scholarship people—we were known as the junior congress—went by bus to Chantilly. We were to dine at a restaurant before proceeding to the famous Stables, where the senior congress was eating. There would be an orchestra and dancing. We were greeted at the restaurant by a brass band of French architecture students wearing what looked like Confederate Army uniforms and playing what might have been national anthems. We were also greeted by a busload of "Parisian models," who were to be our dinner and dancing partners, but that's another story.

After much food and speechifying, torches were passed out. Yes, torches. A few of us—me, the Australians and representatives of other continents—were to climb to the top of the Stables, where there was a microphone and a balcony. The flags of our countries would unfurl as we stepped to the mike to greet our seniors. We would then ask for the lights to be extinguished; the huge doors would swing open, and the rest of the junior congress, the Parisian models and the brass band would march in, all bearing flaming torches.

Ecrasez l'infâme! The mike was dead, the seniors had their heads in champagne buckets and we couldn't get anybody's attention. Thus, when the lights went out and the flaming torches came in, there was pandemonium. Since an insane asylum was known to be in the neighborhood, conclusions were jumped to and people were jumped on.

Worse, when we descended to the floor of the Stables, we learned that to drink champagne we had to have tickets. Six tickets bought a bottle. Nobody had given us any tickets, only torches. And the orchestra wanted to go home. The admirable Australians went into action, table-hopping and glad-handing among the sloshed executives. They came back with baskets of tickets, and the orchestra agreed to play on for a share of the champagne, and we danced until dawn in the Stables of Chantilly, and I swear on my Thesaurus that all of this is true.

Back to Paris at dawn by bus. The Australians wanted to take our dancing partners to Les Halles for a breakfast of white wine and onion soup. This seemed a good idea. Any idea seemed good.

But I couldn't afford it. I excused myself feebly. They insisted. I tried to yawn. They declared a splurge: breakfast was on them. I suspected myself of creepiness. But I went to Les Halles. Who wouldn't? One can't, anymore, because it's gone.

You always remember being a creep. You are reminded in the night.

In London, it would be different. In London, I knew someone to borrow money from. It took me days to find him, and he was not a titan of finance, but he could spare me enough to make possible a night on the town, on me—if I stopped smoking, skipped some meals, didn't tip the chambermaid and slept on the plane home. Our last night, at a discothèque so listless my kneecaps fell off, I flashed my cash.

They wouldn't take it. I explained that I was not a creep. They explained that they were paying. I stamped my foot, which is hard to do without a kneecap. "You are insulting me," said one of the Australians, and he meant it. Who's counting? Who is doing the adding and subtracting? Too right.

I contemplate an anality that has to do with pride instead of money. It is creepy, too.

This Australian who refused my insult is coming to New York, after twelve years of my contemplating. Although I know that he would just as soon sit around listening to Jacques Brel and drinking beer and lamenting the novels we haven't written, I have theater tickets and restaurant reservations and champagne and the firm conviction—not an opinion, a conviction—that he will not insult me by refusing to accept the way we try to say out loud that we are friends.

The Nightcap

He had been to a movie. This was not entirely a mistake, even though they didn't have any buttered popcorn. They didn't have any buttered popcorn because the occasion was a screening. Movies are often screened in New York, in small private theaters without buttered popcorn, for small groups of people who are thought to be opinion makers, before the general public gets its gross chance. All his life he had wanted to be an opinion maker. What fun, to sit in a dark room surrounded by opinions being made. You can hear the brains ticking, like timers for three-minute eggs.

Besides, after the movie they had served wine and cheese, and the cheese had been almost as good as buttered popcorn. It had been better, in fact, than most of what passes for buttered popcorn in the movie houses of this city these days. His buttered popcorn has recently been talking back to him. "Parkay!" it says.

Don't ask what kind of cheese. He doesn't know from cheeses, any more than he knows from cars. If he knew from kinds of cheese and models of cars, there wouldn't be any room left in his head for opinions about movies. And it had been a serious movie.

It was called *Volcano: An Inquiry Into the Life and Death of Malcolm Lowry*. Lowry, of course, spent a lifetime drinking himself to death, and his one great novel, *Under the Volcano*, was also about drinking. The camera, wondering why, was restless—in Mexico, in Canada, in England—while the music swelled and Lowry's words were spoken by Richard Burton, who has known some bottles in his time. People drink themselves to death, and we never know why. Lowry's mother seems not to have loved him much, but according to his brother, their mother didn't love any of her children much. It may be that mothers and fathers are overrated, taking too much credit and being too much blamed for the story of their children. We make our own death.

They talked, after the movie, about Hemingway and Fitzgerald and Faulkner and Lardner and all the other writers who drank too much. Norman Mailer drinks. John Cheever used to. Perhaps, in America at least, the making up and the writing down of stories is understood somehow to be unmanly, and so you drink—and kill animals—as though to grow hair on the chest or the emotions. Or maybe the discrepancies just get to you. This is known as opinion making.

He is home now from the movie. There is a letter from his son waiting for him. His son, a thousand miles away, reports that he is the happiest he has ever been in his fifteen years of life. It is nearly midnight. The father of the happy son thinks that he will fix a nightcap and reread the letter. He knows that he is not responsible for his son's happiness. Friends are responsible, Latin scholars running in a pack on the beaches of Florida, *finally* comradeship, an in-group, telephone calls and plots. But he would like to contemplate his son's happiness, its pure form, the geometry of it, before putting the house to bed.

Even opinion makers need sometimes to be maudlin.

See the bright bottles. They stand in front of a mirror, and are multiplied. They speak in many tongues, and contain flames. There is nothing of the earth that hasn't been distilled. Wheat, corn, rye, oats, rice and potatoes . . . Apples and grapes and pears and plums and juniper berries . . . Molasses and dandelions. Add charcoal or caramel, bubbles or branch water. Everything hops. Except Arabs.

Consider the past, the years of not bruising the vermouth in the pitchers of martinis. (When his mother put him on the plane to college, she explained that there would be social situations where not to drink was impolite, so always order a daiquiri, never accept a martini. An hour after getting off the plane in Boston, he spent the next ten years drinking martinis.) In Havana, covering the revolution and fearing for his hide, he bought Cuba libres— rum and Coca-Cola—for teen-aged *barbudos* with submachine guns in a dive on Malecón Drive. In Paris, in one of the astonishing French supermarkets, he found he could purchase an imperial quart of Scotch at New York prices and deplete it while listening to an Italian opera. In Leningrad, or nearby, on an Intourist bus coming back from a winter palace, he chugalugged enough vodka to make his feet glow through his arctic boots, and had later on to wash his dirty Lenin in public.

We will pass over the eggnog on a New Year's Eve in Larchmont, and several office parties that disclosed a sexual beastliness.

On the other hand, consider his friends. Four of the best of them have dried out in institutions for that purpose, and report regularly to chapter meetings of Alcoholics Anonymous. There are more than nine million alcoholics in this country, and probably fewer than two hundred thousand heroin addicts, depending on how we fudge the stats. His refrigerator is stocked, for his friends, with diet Dr. Pepper, orange juice and apple cider, iced tea. He believes himself immune. Doesn't he, after all, work harder than anybody else? Nightcaps are relaxing. He doesn't need a drink, even though he seems to *want* one most of the time.

Once, as a joke, filling out a questionnaire that asked about his hobbies, knowing that he had none—if he weren't paid to read and write, reading and writing would be his hobbies—he inked in: "I drink." What was he, or Malcolm Lowry, supposed to say? "I make opinions"?

Not really needing a drink, he goes to the kitchen to pop some corn. It won't taste like his youth, and he will boil the butter while trying to melt it, but he achieves a big bowl and munches and contemplates a son who would, in Cuba, be old enough to tote a submachine gun, and who is happy. He manages to finish half of the bowl of popcorn. The person he wants to finish the other half is a thousand miles away.

Now, I am sorry to report, he fixes that nightcap. Nobody's perfect.

The Afghan

This much must be understood about the way they live. Dmitri is a plodder and a slogger. He performs one task at a time, from beginning to end, with the utmost seriousness. There is a time to read and a time to write and a time to change light bulbs. If he is sent to the grocery store, it is best that he be asked to fetch only a few items, and these should be all of one category, like soda crackers or asparagus. To ask him to bring back asparagus and, say, hair shampoo or masking tape is to violate his sense of mission, the purity of the act. While he has been known on Sunday afternoons to combine the watching of professional football with the skimming of a week's batch of magazines, he is not serious on Sunday afternoons. More often, you'll find him in his room, finishing whatever he has started.

He is afraid, of course, that if he nods, if he is distracted, the discrepancies will get him.

Whereas the woman in his life is a nomad and a dervish. She moves from floor to floor and room to room. The house is full of her beginnings and middles. She will leave off reading *The Lay of Igor's Host* to glue a leg on the coffee table. She will, simultaneously, put music on the phonograph, concoct an omelet and place a telephone call. She alternates between working on a crossword puzzle and grading the test papers of her students. She goes out to buy oranges and comes back with an ormolu clock or a petition against plutonium. Mysteriously, by the end of the day, or a week, or at most a month, all that she had begun is somehow done, and a dozen other projects have commenced.

Dmitri thinks of their marriage as a synthesis. Or perhaps it is a syllogism. If it is a syllogism, what is the excluded middle term?

This is nodding. He has allowed himself to become distracted. He ought to be indulging the élite angst for which he is notorious, but the angst rolls off his natural shoulders and forms a pool at his feet and he is thinking about syllogisms. He stares instead at the framed reproduction of Picasso's blind guitar player. It is a relic of his college days, when everybody had framed reproductions from Picasso's blue period, as well as albums of songs by Harry Belafonte. What, Dmitri wonders, is *my* period? Which are my songs? Someone, probably the woman in his life, has stuck a yellow button with black letters into the corner of the frame of the Picasso. It says: MOZART FOREVER. This is unserious.

Renata Adler has reminded us that it is important to be a major character in your own life. She also says: "At six one morning, Will went out in jeans to buy a quart of milk. A tourist bus went by. The megaphone was directed at him. 'There's one,' it said. That was in the 1960's. Ever since, he wondered. There's one what?"

Exactly It seems to Dmitri that it is permissible for him not to understand the 1960's, since the 1950's hadn't understood Dmitri. Now he is in bad shape. Next, he knows, he will start to type, and insist obsessively on trying to justify every line on the right-hand margin of the page. He is stalled in his unseriousness. It is time to talk to the major character in his life.

After a fifteen-minute search, he finds her in his daughter's bedroom. She is surrounded by patches of an afghan, tulip bulbs from Litchfield, Connecticut, and the sermons of Cyril of Turov. She is smoking a crochet hook and reading a modern novel. This is a surprise. She isn't much for modern novels. What have modern novels to do with Russian history and literature, or the French and Chinese revolutions? She marks her place with the crochet hook in the middle of the modern novel, and tosses it aside.

"Listen," she says, "how come it never works out in modern novels? How come they can't hack it? Why are they always disappointed? Why is the center never permitted to hold? Why is love always such a bad trip? Where is it written, except in modern novels, that two people can't get along together? I am tired of the discrepancies."

He is, as usual, grateful to her. She has given him something serious to think about. He sits on Cyril of Turov and stares at the box of tulip bulbs. He will fashion an afghan out of the patches of his angst. It is true that modern novels tell us over and over again that life is impossible. And yet very few people commit suicide. Does this mean that modern novelists are liars, or that most people know more about life than modern novelists, or that sadness sells, or that for a lot of us the impossible is sufficient, is good enough?

A friend of Dmitri's is a poet, and was attacked by a bat in his house in Brooklyn Heights. The bat flew away. Why is it necessary for a modern poet to be attacked by a bat in his own house? Dmitri has never been attacked by a bat in his house. How many depressing poems about bats will result?

To be sure, people who have had difficulties are more interesting than people who have not, and maybe even better. To be sure, too, Western art since the Greeks has mainlined on tragedy. Think of those vehement dithyrambs. But there was something else very Greek that is missing in modern novels, although it isn't missing in Dmitri. It is the notion that we ought to measure ourselves by the intensity and the duration of our lives: intensity *and* duration, passion and stamina. If this is true for the individual, how much more so should it be true for the risk of selves in syntheses or syllogisms like a marriage?

He is prepared to speak his thoughts out loud to the major character in his life. She is not, however, there. He goes from floor to floor and room to room, looking for her. He wants to make an appointment for sex. He finds, in the carriage of his typewriter, a note explaining that she's off to see a Rumanian gymnast at Madison Square Garden, after which she'll stop in on a friend with custody problems before going to the library; and please remember to start the oven at four o'clock. Between now and four o'clock, he can change light bulbs or typewriter ribbons, or watch football and read magazines, or buy masking tape to bind up the discrepancies.

Love

It is later than it should be—at night, in life. Eleven o'clock, and he is still watching a baseball game on television, in the bowels of the house, after the other inmates have gone to bed. Why, he wonders, are the New York Yankees always whining? What liturgical significance attaches to a tantrum? Is Billy Martin necessary?

He is of two minds, or opposing halves of wit. Perhaps he only pretends to enjoy baseball as much as he did back in the days when he had pimples—as if to fool death, as if enthusiasm were a proof of innocence. Perhaps, on the other hand, he is pretending at age thirty-eight to be an adult, an impersonation that obliges him to be suspicious of anything about which other people are enthusiastic. His acne, then, is metaphysical.

It is almost as hard to be enthusiastic as it is to be sincere.

During the commercials, he reads. He is reading famous love letters, which are full of enthusiasm and sincerity. The love letters are collected by Antonia Fraser in a volume called *Love Letters*. It is amusing to look up after reading a letter—from, say, Abélard to Héloïse, or Kafka to Felice, or Count Honoré Gabriel de Mirabeau to Sophie de Monnier—and see Billy Martin throw a tantrum. It is not hilarious, but it is amusing.

However, these letters won't do. The sword of love is dull in print. The surprise and panic, the muscle turned to sponge, the deterioration of one's behavior and one's vocabulary, the fizz and giggles, and bounce and inordinate self-regard are missing. The mystery—why me? why us?—is unelucidated. "Goody, Goody, dear Goody," wrote Jane Welsh Carlyle to Thomas Carlyle, "I have many an anxious thought about you; and I wonder if you sleep at nights, or if you are wandering about—on, on—smoking and killing mice." Whereas Anton Chekhov asked Olga Knipper to "stop spreading melancholera, don't torture me. Be a kind, gentle wife, the kind you really are anyway. I love you more strongly than ever before, and as a husband I am blameless. Why can't you finally understand that, my joy, my little scribble?"

Goody and scribble? Killing mice and spreading melancholera?

Oscar Wilde to Lord Alfred Douglas: "My own dear boy— Your sonnet is quite lovely and it is a marvel that those red rose-leaf lips of yours should be made no less for the music of song than for the madness of kissing." This was not the sort of thing Michael Faraday would have said to Sarah Barnard: "Still, as I ponder and think on you, chlorides, trails, oil, Davy, steel, miscellanea, mercury, and fifty other professional fancies swim before and drive me further and further into the quandary of stupidness." No generalizations are dignified.

Marcel Proust certainly felt bad when he wrote to Madame Straus: ". . . you do not deign to countenance the sentiments which give me the sad rapture of being the most respectful servant of your Sovereign Indifference." But clearly, writing to Mary Anne Wyndham Lewis, Benjamin Disraeli felt worse: "Farewell. I will not affect to wish you happiness for it is not in your nature to obtain it. For a few years you may flutter in some frivolous circle. But the time will come when you will sigh for any heart that could be fond and despair of one that can be faithful. Then will be the penal hour of retribution; then you will recall to your memory the passionate heart that you have forfeited, and the genius you have betrayed."

". . . My mouth is yours," wrote Zelda to Scott Fitzgerald.

"How I wish I could give you a portion of my insensibility!" wrote Nathaniel Hawthorne to Sophia Peabody.

Rosa Luxemburg was easy to please. To Leo Jogiches: "I kiss you a thousand times for your dearest letter and present, though I have not yet received it. . . . You simply cannot imagine how pleased I am with your choice. Why, Rodbertus is simply my favourite economist and I can read him a hundred times for sheer intellectual pleasure."

Wolfgang Amadeus Mozart was easily displeased. To Constanze Weber: "I entreat you, therefore, to ponder and reflect upon the cause of all this unpleasantness, which arose from my being annoyed that you were so impudently inconsiderate as to say to your sisters—and, be it noted, in my presence—that you had let a *chapeau* measure the calves of your legs. No woman who cares for her honour can do such a thing."

Balzac complained to Countess Hanska that "my head is like an empty pumpkin" and "this is the spleen of the heart." He was in better shape than Frédéric Chopin, who worried that his love for Delphine Potocka was bad for his music: "Who knows what ballades, polonaises, perhaps an entire concerto, have been forever engulfed in your little D flat major." (Antonia Fraser explains that D flat major was "their code for the female organ, possibly because D flat is the black key between two white keys C and D.")

And so on. No help at all. The crybabies win the ball game. He must go to his sincere bed enthusiastically, wanting a concerto. Are they really so complicated, being in love and watching baseball? Maybe not. He lives in an age of phone calls instead of love letters, of Astroturf instead of grass, where everybody is a free agent, and he can speak of, by and for only himself, which he does constantly. But on TV and on the street, he is looking and waiting for a grand slam or a triple play, live and in color, spontaneous and improbable and definitive, the opposite of a tantrum.

All right, love. What happens? What has happened to him is that he has grown up, or at least older, like so many men in this country, secretly convinced that he isn't really very interesting. Work, pretending to be an adult, is his way of making himself seem to be interesting. He fears he is commonplace, and will be found out. Then someone explodes on him, someone for whom he is more interesting than anybody else in the park, maybe even *important*, someone who calls him Goody or "my little scribble" and who doesn't notice his metaphysical acne. It is a rally in the ninth inning. He believes her. Why shouldn't he? How couldn't he?

Water Games

We are somewhere in north-central Florida, one of several places airplanes go after they leave Atlanta. It is six-thirty in the morning in a new house with white walls, many windows and sliding glass doors. The sun, taking its time, won't be up for another hour or more, and so we can't see the trees, the plants in their tubs, the flowers in their buckets, the butterflies the size of pancakes, the volleyball net and the hammock that surround the house, nor the black cat with white paws on the roof, wearing what would look like a tuxedo if we snapped an aerial infrared photograph.

At six-thirty in the morning the girl, who will go by bus to school, is still asleep. The boy, who will go by bike, is not. As he moves from his bed to the bathroom to the kitchen, he leaves behind him pools of electric light, footprints of consciousness. He will fetch the newspaper while his bread is toasting. He will sit outside, at a table in a patio, eating toast and reading the newspaper in the light from the kitchen window. The effect, from a distance, is of the house as an aquarium, or of the mundane—breakfast, after all—filmed by a Japanese cameraman underwater through heavy, symbolic lenses.

At seven-twenty the girl gets up to feed herself and the cat. Her brother empties the trash. They strap on book bags, knapsacks, these nomads of knowledge, and are gone before the sun appears. It is a neighborhood in which the sound of the morning is a coughing of cars. Then the day lapses into a kind of parenthesis.

The sidewalks are deserted. Only the birds make noise. Here and there an automatic sprinkler throws a lariat of water on a thriving lawn. Time waits for the children to come home from school, and for the ice-cream truck that will follow them. Should it decide to rain today, the rain will fall at two-fifteen in the afternoon, so as to catch the children on their bikes with their clarinets and their geometry books.

We dreamed this, didn't we—this order, peace and purpose—for ourselves and our children? Our dreamy love goes out, as John Cheever said, "like some limitless discharge of a clear amber fluid that would surround them, cover them, preserve them and leave them insulated but visible like the contents of an aspic."

In such a parenthesis, we can inspect the house. The competence of women is amazing. A year or so ago, this house did not exist. Now it breathes; it has gill . There are boxes of tissues and jars of creams and telephone numbers for emergencies, and a trellis. The wall calendar is oversubscribed with appointments for the dentist, for tennis lessons, for football games. The African figurines seem always to have been on that windowsill, as though limbering up for an aquatic sport.

Like the African figurines, much is familiar. Just as much is strange. The familiar—certain books and pictures, plates, the brand of coffee, a rug, several couches and a record cabinet—stands in unfamiliar light. Perspectives are bent. The piano is against the wrong wall. We are moving sideways, instead of up and down. There is about the familiar objects a sense of prehistory, as if they had been rescued, smuggled out of town, just before the lava flowed down from the terrible mountain.

And yet they are at ease with the strange: the brand of cigarettes, the umbrella stand, the desk, the loft, the Ping-Pong table in the garage, the music on the phonograph. Cooperation abides. Who would have thought those books would have gotten along with that umbrella stand, that from the piano we could see such trees? They partake together of this southern light; they swim in it. Where are the clocks?

The children come home as children do from school, heroic and impatient and hungry and babbling. The boy disappears into his room with his schoolbooks and a bag of pretzels. His sister calls a girlfriend. The friend comes over. They are painting a skeleton on a bedsheet for a Halloween party. As they do so, they discuss the world. For some music, clarinets and pianos and phonographs are not required.

When the phone rings, it is for the boy. And then *his* friend comes over. They are writing a skit for the banquet of their Latin

Forum. It is full of puns on the order of "forum and against 'em." Drunk on themselves, they stagger into the living room to read aloud and heehaw. Did the Romans enjoy themselves so much? The Greeks probably had more fun. But the Greeks were serious, too. They played games and wrote tragedies.

We will eat outside tonight, off familiar plates in the unfamiliar patio, in the vicinity of the barbecue grill. Because their mother has gone to Washington on business, we will see to it that they consume green beans and milk with their meat, and apples afterward. The boy will then again go off by bike path to his high school for a competition so elaborate—they are refighting the Punic Wars—that no description, even if it were possible, is advisable. We will play Scrabble and poker, and watch television, with his sister. She will go to bed with James Thurber and a transistor radio. Much later, her brother will go to bed with Arthur Koestler's *The Thirteenth Tribe*—not that, in his busy schedule, he has time for bed, but he must go there in order overnight to grow another foot.

Now the new house is a submarine in the deep night, with only a pilot light. See it snooze sleekly. What is the matter with this picture of the water games of the middle class? Just one thing. The father of these children is in north-central Florida for five days of babysitting—as though they were babies, as though they ever sat—because their mother is in Washington for five days of business. Their father sleeps in the guest room of the new house with an open suitcase.

Don't Tell My Friends

They are coming from all over, by cab and helicopter and rubber duck, for the opera and for professional meetings and for Thanksgiving and for the hell of it. This is the season; New York is Oz. We need, in the hallway or on the roof, one of those carrousels for luggage. We also need an espresso bar and a liquor license. One of the many advantages of living in New York, as of living in Paris, is that your friends will find you. You are on their map.

Variously bandaged, they bring trophies from foreign campaigns. In their bags of bones are anecdotes and compromises, missals and ears. We seem somehow never to get out of the kitchen, and when the phone rings it is not for me. Standing at the kitchen window, looking down at the garden, which is full of yellow leaves, I think that my past is a tree and that every autumn it drops my friends on me; they fall in my space. It is as if, from these leaves, from this talk, we are trying to make a quilt to warm us for the winter, or maybe a rainbow. Listen to them. One friend doesn't drink coffee. What, then, is her substitute for caffeine on those late nights when she needs to work, or those cold early mornings when she can't get her head started? She considers the question. She replies: "I eat a raisin."

Another reminisces of his days in radio. He was in Miami for the Republican Convention of 1972. He recorded an improbable conversation between Mr. Nixon's favorite rabbi, Baruch Korf, and Colonel Sanders of Kentucky. For thirty-five minutes they talked about the feasibility of marketing kosher fried chicken nationwide.

A third, a professor at a university down South, has been impressed, and perhaps a little frightened, by the healthy good looks of the female undergraduates. One of them had apologized to him for not being able to join his seminar in the fall semester, asking if he would promise to save a place for her in the spring.

"Save a place for her?" he asks. "What *wouldn't* I have done for her?" He thinks about it. Not even these low decades have coarsened him. "I would," he said, "I would . . . I would have carried her books all the way across campus."

It is my turn to paddle on this gentle pond. I tell of having gone the other night to a delicatessen to purchase a sandwich, which I intended to eat while watching the World Series. I ordered a roast beef on a roll. What would I like on it? "Butter," I replied recklessly. The man behind the counter shook his head. Indeed, the entire delicatessen was as silent as the inside of a shoe. How had I offended? Of course; this was a kosher delicatessen. I had lived in this city for ten years, and the woman in my life was Jewish, and I had proposed, under the fiery eye of God, to mix a meat product with a dairy product. The man behind the counter said: "I won't put anything on it. Take it away. We'll never know what you do to it when you get it home where we can't see you."

Embarrassment is one of my categories. Maybe next week I will write a column on embarrassment.

And so we sit in the kitchen as though it were a canoe, under moon lamps. They have initiated, or removed, beards. They have stopped, or resumed, smoking. Their children are brave or dangerous. Their books are going well or have been abandoned. Their teeth, feet, mortgages and principles are bothering them. Souls of kindness, they affirm a solidarity. Tinker with ourselves as we may, as if we were chunks of sentient clay, we are for the moment as young as we used to be, when making friends was easy, when adulthood was some movie we could still walk out on.

I am pleased.

Then why is it, tonight of all nights, that they are dispersed? Why have they all gone to a theater or a concert or a lecture or a wake? Why is the eleven-year-old, who—because of weeks of late nights with old friends and older anecdotes, because of sleepy days at school—was put to bed at eight o'clock, now in our living room in pain? Foolishly, she has been playing in bed with a ring that doesn't belong to her. Foolishly, she has forced the ring down over her knuckle. She ought to have known that it is in the nature of knuckles to work in only one direction: down the finger, not up. She can't get the ring off.

And the knuckle is swollen. And the finger looks like a sausage. And soap doesn't help, and neither does ice, and what doesn't hurt is numb, and the various people in this city who always know what to do in any sort of emergency aren't answering their telephones. Where are they, anyway? At the library, or in night school, learning how to cope? Is there an all-night jewelry store in the neighborhood, where we could get the ring off? Whoever heard of an all-night jewelry store?

This finger will not last until morning. I contemplate our tools: a pair of pliers, a monkey wrench, a carving knife, a can opener. It is in the nature of tools to be adequate only for the previous emergency. Had I a hacksaw, I wouldn't know how to use it. I do not cope; I type. Where is everybody? Stop the movie; I want to be innocent. I promise never again to put butter on roast beef. I will eat raisins instead.

Why does it take me half an hour to think of calling the hospital around the corner? The hospital tells us to try soap and ice. But we have. Well, then, bring her in and we'll use the ring cutter. Of course, hospitals specialize in ring cutters. She is brought in; the ring is cut off. She goes to bed at eleven instead of eight o'clock. I swear her to secrecy. Don't tell my friends. I am a New Yorker, and they think I'm an adult.

Three Truths

Were we to look at the living room with the same sharp eye for symbols that we bring, say, to a Russian triptych, we might find something of iconographic significance. Then again, we might not. On the left is a daguerreotype; on the right, an ashtray and a bottle; to the north, books; to the south, sound. In the middle, a man lies on the floor on his back with his head on a pillow, listening in the gloom of the evening to Cat Stevens. His hands are folded on his stomach, as if he were about to be tucked away in a bureau drawer or a crypt. From God's point of view, he is a clock stopped at six. Anthropologists and astronauts will have to tell us whether tennis courts, bathtubs and men on living-room floors are all laid out in the same direction.

Why is this man listening to Cat Stevens? Why, before Cat Stevens, was he listening to Janis Ian? And why, after Cat Stevens, will he listen to Phoebe Snow, when he should instead be reading Lawrence Stone on *The Family, Sex and Marriage* in England from 1500 to 1800, or adding heartburn to the chili?

As a matter of fact, earlier in the gloaming, he had tried to listen to Peter Frampton and Steely Dan, but he couldn't understand their noises. Being a word man—because words are guilty of association with rational comment and abstract ideas—he insists on knowing what's going on. Not what's going down, but *on*. Except in the case of opera, especially those by Wagner. It had been a mistake to learn what was going on in Wagner. As Mark Twain remarked after a performance of *Lohengrin*, "The banging and slamming and booming and crashing were something beyond belief."

Cat Stevens sings "Father & Son." It is not Turgenev, but the man on the floor thinks it is very nice, as he had thought Janis Ian's singing "In the Winter" was very nice, as he will think Phoebe Snow's singing whatever she wants to very nice.

He listens to these people sing as part of a cram course in popular culture in order to prepare himself for meeting the young. He will be meeting the young, in the form of a tribe of talented college freshmen, in a couple of days, for dinner. They will ask him questions. That is the purpose of the dinner. He knows where the anecdotes are buried. He is, as he nears the end of his fourth decade, a resource material, an anthology with the thumbprints of many institutions on his cover and spine.

And yet he is worried. The young come from another country, a third kingdom. They seethe with popular culture. They eat television for breakfast. They are plugged into energy sockets, wired for metaphors, of which he is innocent. His hallucinations (political, bookish) and theirs (musical, cinematic) are out of phase. They speak a different anguish. He looks, with his ear as an eye, at their culture for evidence of common chords: stamina, reciprocity, the idea in modulation, caring, citizenship, nuance.

He finds, between big beats, such evidence. He is nonetheless a whisk broom of nerves, scattering rather than combining his sensations. Should he, for instance, wear a tie to this dinner? Although he almost never wears a tie, he owns one. He will wear it, like the diseased tongue it seems to him to be, because to do otherwise would in some way misrepresent the distance he feels between their kingdom and his. He wouldn't want to give them the impression that he was laid back, even if he is on his back listening to Cat Stevens.

On the other hand—and he has many more hands than a clock —to wear a tie is to impersonate the adult he has never quite been sure he is. He is fond of observing that character is the accumulation of painful experiences. Such an assertion presupposes that on the adding machine of ourselves we have a total-bar. Is this true in the kingdom of the young? Ought he pretend to be an adult, or a comrade? The tennis courts and bathtubs of his mind are at right angles.

It is all very well for Phoebe Snow to stand up on the rock. When he stands up, it is on a Prufrock. Is laid back the same thing as being etherized?

He will wear the tie. So, amazingly, will they, as if to signify

seriousness, as though tethered to a hitching post on Morningside Heights to eat his oats instead of television. They will be
handsome and clever, and he will not egregiously embarrass himself, although a sense of his own babbling will sneak up on him
and he will not sound, in his own head, as nice as Cat Stevens. He
will keep changing the cassette in his skull. Loudspeak.

Still, these freshmen will be only three years older than his
own son. And when the man on the floor was a freshman at college, twenty-one years ago, he had to wear a tie to every meal in
the dining hall. He stuffed spoons and forks into the breast pocket
of his tweed jacket, the better to dismember the remarks of his
professors on Prufrock and triptychs. He had never rented a hotel
room, or gone to a funeral, or betrayed a confidence. He knew
nothing of the surpassing generosity of women. He loitered in the
vicinity of his life.

His children: does he babble at them as he will to college
freshmen, so much information overload, so little wisdom? Has
he never sung? He will descend from Morningside Heights, qualm
by qualm, to a cab. How wise is this guy? He will wonder whether
he should have told these young, handsome and clever people the
few truths that sing in his bones. These are:

1. Nobody can ever get too much approval.

2. No matter how much you want or need, *they*, whoever *they*
are, don't want to let you get away with *it*, whatever *it* is.

3. Sometimes you get away with it.

Faces

The great man was comfortable inside his face. He wore his face like a shoe, a hiking boot; they had been some places together, and heard some music. The great ones, men and women, often have such faces, as if custom-made, with the grain showing, old leather on which we strop ourselves, acquire our edge. We sit around them at a dinner table, or in a private room in a midtown club, over coffee and cognac, talking about art or economics. They never have to think of an expression to put on. They have produced books and grandchildren and these faces, and that is sufficient. Their bones are their expression.

Rainer Maria Rilke was wrong in *The Notebooks of Malte Laurids Brigge*. Or Malte, in Paris at the turn of the century, looked in the wrong places for his faces. "There are people," he confided to his notebook,

who wear the same face for years; naturally it wears out, it gets dirty, it splits at the folds, it stretches, like gloves one has worn on a journey. These are simple, thrifty people; they do not change their face, they never even have it cleaned. It is good enough, they say, and who can prove to them the contrary? The question of course arises, since they have several faces, what do they do with the others? They store them up. Their children will wear them. But sometimes, too, it happens that their dogs go out with them on.

Then, again:

Other people put their faces on, one after the other, with uncanny rapidity and wear them out. At first it seems to them they are provided for always; but they scarcely reach forty—and they have come to the last. This naturally has something tragic. They are not accustomed to taking care of faces; their last is worn through in a week, has holes, and in many places is thin as paper; and then, little by little, the under layer, the no-face, comes through, and they go about with that.

Finally:

The woman startled and pulled too quickly out of herself, too violently, so that her face remained in her two hands. I could see it lying in them, its hollow form. It cost me indescribable effort to stay with those hands and not to look at what had torn itself out of them. I shuddered to see a face from the inside, but still I was much more afraid of the naked flayed head without a face.

It seems to me that Malte, like so many characters in the modern literature of fire alarms, of exacerbations, goes about perceiving everything backward. Feeling bad, wherever he looks he sees mirrors full of bad feeling, weepy windows when the rain is all inside. If his gloves, and his thin paper full of holes, and his hollow form and flayed head are wrong, I suppose my shoes and strop are wrong, too. We grow our faces. "A man of fifty," said Edwin M. Stanton, "is responsible for his face." Yes, and a woman of fifty as well, even if she has made an appointment for her face with a knife.

The great man explained inflation and the exchange rate. He discussed cows in Switzerland and Arthur F. Burns at the Federal Reserve Board. He enjoyed being a great man, as who wouldn't? I enjoy the company of people who enjoy being themselves, whether great or merely beautiful. We are told that having to be great and beautiful all the time can be a burden, but I would prefer not to think so, and don't believe it. We need the great and the beautiful, those occasions for applause. I cannot feel altogether bad about a world that contains, for example, Blythe Danner. I sat there, growing my face.

And later, walking home in the usual monsoon, I remembered a photograph and wondered if it was still in my possession. It had been snapped in 1956 in southern California: me, at age seventeen, shaking hands with Adlai Stevenson, my first great man, the proudest moment of my life. I had just introduced him to a convention of Young Democrats. Surely, by 1956, the Governor had already grown his face, while I was merely starting out on mine. The incipient self.

I couldn't find the photograph. My desk is a slum and the old wooden filing cabinet is nothing more than a gigantic wastepaper basket full of guilt—hundreds of pictures of children and friends, hundreds of letters from strangers. When you write in public about children and friends (and cats), people write back. They write generous and astonishing letters in whose pages faces grow, histories are told. I am dumbfounded. It is impossible for me to write, even to my mother, without a deadline, and yet the room swells with other people's emotions, as though the books on the shelves had opened up, as if they were singing. I haven't any answers; the great and the beautiful have answers and secretaries.

And the pictures. See the faces grow, out of innocence into guile, the unnecessary squint, wonderment and superstition, the shadow of doubt, maybe, why not, old marriages, abandoned rooms, a tennis court, an apple tree, one dog, one clarinet, aviator goggles, falling leaves and hair, ceremony, scandal. It is a city, a Paris, of faces. The attic of me isn't big enough to contain them. The children swim, elongating, through their history, toward their faces. Of course they will be great and beautiful. Greatness and beauty always skip a generation.

I couldn't find Adlai Stevenson or my father.

My family found me, under the filing cabinet, surrounded by letters from strangers and pictures of friends. Having been out themselves, in the monsoon, their faces were wet and so they probably wouldn't have been able to tell whether mine was or not, even if they could have seen it, which they couldn't have because it was in my hands, where, I am happy to report, it didn't wear out or come off. Grow, I told my face. In time, my face replied.

Snapshots

We sat in one of the several dining rooms in the grand hotel under a vaulted ceiling. Somebody else could tell you about the wooden ribs on that ceiling, but I am the sort of person who doesn't know an ogive from a tierceron or, for that matter, a Ford from a Chevrolet. Besides, while with appropriate seriousness my friend and I drank beer, yonder, through glass doors, on the other side of the beach, the Pacific Ocean was being exhibitionistic.

My friend had been reading René Dubos. He explained: "The process of converting barley into beer involved physicists in the problems of gas pressure, chemists in the structure of starch, enzymologists in the mechanisms of fermentation, and micro-biologists in the study of yeasts and bacteria." We were grateful, and not at all sobered by the thought of how important beer had been in the development of European science.

I am going to say that my friend is French, although he may not be. We were freshpersons together at college. In those days, he was a poet, in the manner of Jules Laforgue. In those days, I was a lout, in the manner of the North Beach Beats with whom I had trafficked. (If a snob imitates the manners of the class above him, a bohemian imitates the manners of the class below him.) Later, I would resort to journalism, and he would disappear into the academy.

But before he disappeared, he came to my wedding. His gift was a hammock, a big canvas hammock wrapped up in a bundle the size of a canoe. For a couple of newlyweds on their way to a two-room apartment in Manhattan, such a hammock may have seemed a problematical wedding present. I remember feeling at the time, though, that only a poet could have thought of it.

He was gone for fifteen years. Or: I was gone, and he was there, wherever he happened to be. I heard that he was abroad; that he had gone West; that he had married; that he was no longer married; that he had become a professor at one of those California universities that spring up overnight like shopping malls; that he was writing a novel. I no longer had the hammock or the marriage, but I was in California and I called.

My friend is happy. One can tell: a new marriage, a small child and many color snapshots. He was, in fact, padded with packets of photographs, and came to lunch armed with a camera. Photography seems to have occurred to him several years ago, perhaps at the onset of the new marriage, as if he were collecting evidence of his happiness to show to his friends. I don't take pictures; I've always thought that it is the purpose of grandmothers to photograph one's children, and that mountains and cathedrals are tired of having to look at cameras. I saw, however, in the grand hotel that there was something miserly in my attitude; I wanted to hoard, instead of sharing, my impressions and experiences. There may also have been something arrogant about supposing that my typewriter was better than a camera.

After finishing our beer, we walked on the beach. It is impossible on a California beach to feel very much like Stephen Dedalus. All is so clean that you feel more like the Good Humor man. Or, on this particular beach in front of the grand hotel, with fountains to the right and tennis courts to the left, like one of the insubstantial zombies from *Last Year at Marienbad*. Here my friend took my picture. I was sure the developing fluid would dissolve me, that between the vault and the sea there would be nothing, certainly not nimbus, not even a shadow, just blank space. We take ourselves far too seriously if we imagine the universe could be bothered to erase us from a snapshot.

And then, on the way back to his car, my happy friend told me his story. I will omit the artful details, because for all I know he may be using them in the novel he has written. But it went, roughly, like this:

Seven years ago my friend went back to, well, France, in some confusion as to where, in which country, his future lay. There were also complications having to do with his father's business and estate. The more he immersed himself in those complications, the more confused he became. The truth, as we were promised when we were young, will sometimes out.

It seems that my friend's father, the only father he had ever known, was not his biological father. His biological father had died, heroically, in one of the wars. His mother, pregnant and widowed, remarried. For various reasons belonging to his novel and not to this article, my friend was never advised of these facts until, as a grown man, he had to understand them in order to sort out the complications of the business and the estate.

Not only hadn't he known of his biological father, but he was wholly unaware of a set of relatives, dozens of them, on that father's side of the family. My friend, who had never even seen a photograph of his own father, had aunts and uncles and cousins who had followed his career from childhood through college and graduate school and a marriage and professoring. They had albums full of him, and he had been ignorant of their existence.

I understand the camera now. You see: we exist, come and go, grow and die; it has been recorded.

How do you like that gas, starch, yeast, bacteria and fermentation, those ogives and tiercerons? In the parking lot, under that sun, what a novel! And, wretch that I am, merchant of psychic yard goods, peddler of scrimshaw, I envied him. He was born interesting. He didn't have to invent himself. How come some people get all the ambivalence, while the rest of us have to work at it?

So I'm stealing his story.

On Being Embarrassed

According to William Blake: "The bird a nest, the spider a web, man friendship." Dmitri was happily surrounded by his favorite novelist, his favorite teacher, his favorite film writer, his favorite literary critic and his favorite folk singer. The teacher, of course, came with the franchise. How the others had all managed to be together in the same room, Dmitri's cave, is a mystery, but one that he embraced. Dmitri and the literary critic were the only men, because this is New York. Only the literary critic wore shoes, because, as we know, literary critics are the vanguard of civilization. It is as if a living room, any living room, were the seventeenth-century Peking court of K'ang Hsi and the critic a Portuguese Jesuit just come from Europe with the Word.

Anyway, for the evening, Dmitri's favoritism was an aspic, containing the eggs of their excellence. Any worry that they might have found themselves too good for one another, that so much separate wit would add up to an occlusion, had vanished with the garlic at the dinner table. The smokers now blew smoke out the window so as not to offend the nonsmokers.

They talked of embarrassment. This talk was not psychologized chichi, the loose change left in the libidinal cash register after all the big bills had been removed by a Freudian or a Jungian or a Sullivanian analyst. (Analysis for the moment seems to be out of fashion in New York. In fashion are horses and ballet.) Nor was it pop-therapeutic word flab from the pits of est. (Dmitri wouldn't allow such people into his house. They frightened the horses.) It was, instead, anecdotal, *sans-façon*, a slow spoon river of situations badly handled, pratfalls, unseemliness. A surprisingly large number of these anecdotes had to do with incontinence or sexual ambiguity—which proves, if anything, that we have come far enough in our brave new world to speak of such matters without blushing. The Freudians believe that blushing is a mild form of conversion hysteria, an erection of the entire head. Dmitri believes that, in our brave new world, blushing is a form of nostalgia. It is not known what the horses, the Jesuits and K'ang Hsi believe.

There were also doctor stories, which are usually embarrassing. For reasons made clear in feminist literature, women seem to have a worse time with doctors than men do. Maybe men have less trouble, too, because they go to doctors less often. Dmitri had gone recently to a doctor to discourage a variety of exotic diseases, and for the dreaded physical examination. Of physical examinations, a male friend had declared: "The only one I want is an autopsy."

But Dmitri, having avoided a medical checkup for years, felt obliged to go. Why, then, had he wanted to lie to the doctor about all his bad habits? A doctor's office isn't an encounter group, or even a newspaper pub. You can't invent yourself as you maunder on. Your fabrications aren't going to impress the blood test, the urinalysis or the chest X-ray. Science is not amused. To lie to a doctor is not an embarrassment; it's an insanity. Dmitri, admitting that he had defiled the temple of his body, spilled various beans.

Science is probably not amused, either, that Dmitri seems to be healthy. Reason itself is offended.

A happy, healthy, shoeless and unblushing Dmitri put Judy Collins on the phonograph:

> *Open the door and come on in*
> *I'm so glad to see you, my friend.*
> *You're like the rainbow comin' around the bend*
> *And when I see you happy,*
> *Well, it sets my heart free.*
> *I'd like to be as good a friend to you*
> *As you are to me.*

His rainbows, his favorites, were deeper into embarrassment. Their habit was to pounce on the skittering nuance. Surely, they decided, there were embarrassments more serious than not making it to the bathroom in time. Incontinence and sexual ambiguity were kid stuff. Their memory didn't keep you awake at night, or sweat the fat out of your self-esteem, or freeze the glands. You could turn them into anecdotes, whereas profound embarrassment requires a novel. You can hide in a novel, among extenuating circumstances.

What about the unnecessary wound, the sick joke, cravenness at a time of crisis, indifference in a time of need, ambition put before friendship? In profound embarrassment there was something dishonorable, a cowardly seed, a secret betrayal. Who, besides God, are we afraid to face, whether they care any longer or not about what we did or failed to do? The ones who have measured us, and found us wanting—they are the guerrillas of embarrassment; they strike by night, wearing mirrors instead of pajamas.

Wasn't this sort of embarrassment just another word for shame or guilt? Well, one has to begin somewhere. We have, in the brave new world, passed a resolution against embarrassment, shame and guilt. The Word, from California instead of Europe, allows us to let it all hang out. The Word is a gallows tree. Our secret knowledge, down there with the secret betrayals, is that to be capable of embarrassment is the beginning of moral consciousness. Honor grows from qualms. Dmitri's favorites, except for the teacher, staggered into the night. Soon he would be leaving alone, by plane not horse, for the mysterious East, out of the nest and the web. He realized that he had gone to his friends, as he had gone to the doctor, for an inoculation. Against what? Please, sir, in the court of K'ang Hsi, let me not embarrass myself. But he always had, and he would probably come back once again with anecdotes instead of a novel. It is not invariably easy to have smart friends.

White Tigers

We must put up for a while with Dmitri's journey to the East. At least he went without Hermann Hesse, who causes pimples. (The only thing in Dmitri's bag was ignorance, like a portable precipice.) And he hadn't gone, like André Malraux, to steal Cambodian art. (If he could bring back one work of art from the Orient, it would be the women.) He was there to talk about literature. He had been talking, day and night, for two weeks, with another week to go.

Two nights before this morning, he had been, implausibly, to dinner in a palace of culture on the landfill in Manila Bay. The dinner was to honor a group of Swedish directors in the Philippines for a film festival, and to appease a group of writers in transit to Australia for the meetings of International P.E.N. To Dmitri's left sat the bearded director of *I Am Curious Yellow.* To his right sat the clean-shaven Peruvian novelist Mario Vargas Llosa. Drinking British whiskey, waving silver chopsticks, thousands of miles away from Stockholm, Lima and New York, far above the gunboats and the gambling casinos floating in the bay, they had discussed Sinclair Lewis. The world is a serious place.

Two nights after this morning, he would be, blearily, in front of a hotel in the middle of Seoul. The hotel stands just across a traffic jam from Duksu Palace. There would be no traffic jam, however, because the time would be a minute after the midnight curfew, and the city would have abolished itself, rescinded its breathing; and the hotel would silently advance on him, like a great ship or a floating palace, on engines of light; and he would remember, weak-kneed, a moment in the evening—an evening that began with Korean rice wine and gobbets of octopus in warm stalls resembling subway cars, an evening that would go on to a "salon" in which he sat shoeless while young women of refinement poured his drinks, lit his cigarettes and touched his thigh—when he rose to a microphone and sang, for the cause of cultural exchange, several verses of Algernon Charles Swinburne's "Garden of Proserpine."

Swinburne is serious, too, like the world and Sinclair Lewis. Even Dmitri is serious, although not when he sings in salons.

But this morning he is in the mountains, hours to the south of Seoul. He has gone by train to Taegu and by car with new friends from Taegu to the mountains, where the white tigers of Korean art are said to dwell. December is a brown time for Korea. You should see it, say his friends, with flowers: the cherry trees, the apple orchards and the golden rice. Besides the blue sky, the brown earth and the green pines, the only color is to be found on the tin roofs of the village shacks, which are too bright, like advertisements for newness.

Dmitri would have preferred the thatched roofs of the old Korea, but one must get out of the habit of thinking of other cultures as gift shops for tourists.

Nevertheless, the land: every inch of it is cultivated. Terraces rise to the mountains, and seem to hang in their intricacy. The agriculture is itself an art, working with height and contour and correspondences, manicured. It is signed with a plow. It follows a grain, a logic. It isn't fussy or tricky, like Japanese gardens. Bamboo hoops seem to be waiting for a game of croquet to begin.

They reach the sacred ground, where the pines are dying and the white tigers are hiding. Beyond a school, a gas station and a gift shop, a footpath winds up to the temple of Haein-sa. At the gate to the temple is a steep ascent of steps. These, too, have been terraced. Here, a garden; there, a shrine, a meditation room, a hermitage with, incredibly, a television antenna. Hardly anyone else is about. Dmitri climbs a thousand years into the past.

As they enter what seems to be the main courtyard of the temple, a gong is struck, sticks are rattled and a huge suspended drum goes to work, sounding rather Navajo and jazzy. The monks are summoned to their golden Buddhas for devotions. Like the Peruvian novelist, they are clean-shaven, even their heads. Last night was a full moon, the only time of the month they are allowed to shave. They ignore Dmitri, whose Western head is heavy with used words.

Higher, then, to the library. The library contains the Pal-man-dae-jang-gyung. A plaque explains that the Pal-man-dae-jang-gyung is a complete set of the Buddhist scriptures, the entire literature of a religion and a civilization, hand-carved by monks on wooden blocks in Sanskrit and Chinese characters. There are 81,258 such wooden blocks in the library. When the Mongols destroyed one library, the monks started carving all over again, and finished this set three hundred years later, in 1251, two centuries before Gutenberg.

Dmitri is out of words. They look for water. A monk—the librarian?—leads them to a well. They pester him with questions. Their excitement is contagious. A happy man, he unlocks the doors to the library, invites them into the stacks, permits them to hold a wooden block in their hands. Understand that these are *printing* blocks. Each of the three hundred characters on each face of each block has been carved backward, so that ink can be applied and a page printed on paper. Dmitri, who has come to Asia to talk about literature, who has in a temple on a Korean mountaintop held in his hands a literature that makes Sinclair Lewis and Algernon Swinburne seem unserious, feels like the drum in the courtyard, and the gong.

The happy monk hands Dmitri a name card. Dmitri is the only man in Asia without cards with his name on them. The monk disappears. Dmitri stands in the sun looking down the terraces of the sacred ground. In ten minutes the monk is back, with what seems to be a scroll, wrapped in newspaper, tied with a pink ribbon. The monk has caused to be printed three pages of the Pal-man-dae-jang-gyung from wooden blocks carved by men of faith eight hundred years ago. These are a gift for Dmitri.

What does one say to such a gift? It occurs to Dmitri, helplessly, to say to the monk and to the white tigers and to Asia and to everybody: Merry Christmas.

Dash

Had he felt an epiphany coming on, he might have been able to time it better. New Year's Eve, after all, has no other discernible purpose. How nice it would have been for such a seizure to coincide with the falling of the ball down Times Tower, like an aspirin tablet in the esophagus of history. "Doctor," says the Old Year, "my minutes leak and my months ache." "Take two Lombardos, my son, and call me after the football game."

But the epiphany sneaked up on him, and so he was two hours late. This was in a house in Manhattan. The house was full of children, and their parents, and their grandparents—assorted and amiable riffraff, all of whom agreed that New Year's Eve is a bad idea, especially if it includes babysitters. And so they had gathered together, with their hostages, to listen to music and to play Bingo and to drink champagne.

The champagne, admittedly, was a bargain-basement brand. Does anyone remember the television commercial for "the champagne of bottled beers"? Well, this was the beer of bottled champagnes. It was nevertheless consumed, and the children were fierce in the dying light of the year, and their parents—like elm trees or elks with palmate antlers—looked down with heavy heads at their mysterious play.

Now the television set and the record player were switched off; the Bingo chips had been ground into the carpet; and the children were asleep, rolled up like pairs of socks or hand grenades in the various drawers of the house. The elks were at the round table in the kitchen, wondering if there was anything else they could do to postpone going back to whatever they had done, with brave monotony, before. How, in other words, to prolong this parenthesis?

Ordinarily, at such a time, he would have called his mother in California: Although Guy Lombardo is dead, I am not. But his mother wasn't in California. She was on board a ship somewhere between New Orleans and Yucatán. What a dashing thing to do, spending Christmas and New Year's in the Gulf of Mexico, between the ghost towns of French and Mayan civilizations. There had been little enough dash in her life, not nearly as much as she deserved—one trip to Europe, a cabin in the mountains, a political convention in Chicago where she had been pledged to the vanished candidacy of Robert F. Kennedy. Some people make money; others make friends. She would by now have made a boatload of new friends.

He approved of his mother, and wished her a dashing new year. Odd, though, the way the web of the mind catches flies. Just this summer in the mountains, looking at an album of the sort of old photographs that make the past difficult to take seriously, his mother and he had arrived at a secret. Not a dark secret: it had, in fact, white teeth and dimples. It was a very handsome secret. It was a snapshot of the young European diplomat his mother might have married shortly after the end of World War II.

He would have been eight, and his younger brother four, when the diplomat left Washington, D.C., by plane, to go back to Europe, and his mother left Washington, D.C., by train, for the great unknown of southern California. He could remember, vaguely, the handsome, friendly face with the white teeth; and a roadster, maybe even with a rumble seat; and a sled on a snowbank; and probably, the inexplicable electricity of sexual tension. He had wondered over the years, after he had gotten a toehold on adult realities, about that diplomat. He had never underestimated his mother.

But he hadn't known until this summer that marriage had been formally proposed; that a round-trip ticket to Paris had been proffered, just to give his mother a sense of what the Continent was like, and that the ticket and the marriage had been refused. Why? Well, against his grandmother's wishes and knowledge, his mother had eloped before the war, and the marriage had been a sad bust. The time, the next time, perhaps the wrong time, his mother had sought and accepted his grandmother's advice, and gone in the other direction from Europe.

She wouldn't, in fact, get to Europe for another twenty-five years, and then it rained for three weeks, which in no way diminished her dash.

To learn that your future was decided thirty years ago on the basis of problematical advice from your grandmother, who has for more than twenty years been correcting God's spelling, is to be tickled or cuffed by the wing of fate, and to feel not a little helpless. He thought about it on the first day of the new year. The diplomat had gone on, in the service of his country, to all the capitals of Europe, and to the Orient. A stepchild might have mastered, instead of mangling, several languages; could have made friends with the Alps and the Louvre; would have had an education instead of an apprenticeship according to whose austere terms one learns how to climb out of the lower middle class and purport to be a gentleman.

And the mother of the child might have lived in those castles instead of looking at them in picture books; could have written novels instead of typing correspondence; would have been worth a great deal more to postwar Europe than the Marshall Plan.

Ah, but here comes the tardy epiphany. The mother of the child would not now be in the Gulf of Mexico with the man she loves. The child would not now be in this house, with his own children, and there is no other place he wants to be. He would like to have arrived here via Europe, but not to have risked ending up anywhere else. Isn't it amazing the way the future succeeds in creating an appropriate past? One allows oneself, perhaps dangerously, as the new year brushes its teeth, to conclude that one must be happy, and to hope that it will be contagious.

Interior Monologue

We didn't take the children to the nightclub the other Friday night. Who knows whether children are even allowed in nightclubs, although nightclub furniture—those tables the size of hubcaps—seems to have been pillaged from a kindergarten class in Lilliput, designed for munchkins with credit cards.

I had enough trouble taking myself to a nightclub. For one reason or another—maybe it was being born at an early age, or the wrong one; maybe it was laziness or lack of imagination; maybe it was the diet of a bookworm—I did not grow up going to nightclubs, or beach parties, or coffeehouses, or any other service station of the libido. It was all I could do to go to schools and movies. I was in Las Vegas once, for twenty-four hours, which was like being trapped inside Dean Martin's cerebellum with a bunch of omophagous lizards.

But we had other reasons for not taking the children. Not so long ago we took the children to the Pete Seeger concert at Carnegie Hall. This was supposed to be a treat. What, then, did they think of Pete Seeger? Well, they said, he was okay. "Okay" in the mouths of the children around here means, "Look, I don't really want to hurt your feelings, but . . ." They hurt my feelings. They didn't much care for Pete Seeger's voice.

His *voice*. The impertinence. Stick it in your ear and see if it sharpens; you're missing the point. With all the cunning at the command of someone who has been a father for fifteen years, I said I supposed that they preferred the *voice* of, say, Bob Dylan. As a matter of fact, they replied, they didn't much care for Bob Dylan's voice, either. They liked his songs better when somebody else sang them.

Bring back Snooky Lamson. Children are overrated. The next time I take them anywhere, it will be to a bus terminal.

I lie of course. We went to the nightclub without the children because, I think, in a way we were scared. It was opening night for Mort Sahl at Dangerfield's on the Upper East Side near all the hospitals. We, the children of the 1950's, were scared that Sahl might bomb. His comeback was important to us, but if he did bomb, we did not want the children of the 1970's sitting around looking at us as though we had water on the brain or Ovaltine in our varicose veins.

Is it necessary to explain why Mort Sahl was important to us? That would require going back twenty years to a time when all the comedians had keys in their backs, when all the jokes were about mothers-in-law and mammary glands, when it wasn't even possible to imagine a Lily Tomlin. Then, while we were in college, along came people like Mort Sahl and Lenny Bruce, and it was as if they had been reading our thoughts; they had been down and out in anxiety and paranoia. They were scourges, yes, but they represented something more as well—an amalgam of the rogue poetry of Provence, the interior monologues of Joyce, the babble of the analysand, the long nights of radio and the static in the cavities of our teeth.

There are too many assistant professors of Lenny Bruce for me to dare to generalize on his miserable life and ugly death. But Mort Sahl: with his Joe College looks, his open collar and V-neck sweater, his newspapers and his qualms and his iconoclastic politics—he was our edgy stand-in, our chevalier, Huck Finn with a ball-point mind. He rambled and he scored, and his heh-heh was indeed a black gurgle, as though he were laughing himself to death at all that he knew. History resents such guys.

He went strange after the assassination of John Kennedy. And in that sense, too, he was a stand-in for the children of the 1950's. It suddenly seemed that we were no longer the pampered children of the Enlightenment, getting better every day. Until that particular assassination, there was a European way of thinking about conspiracies (there has to be a conspiracy, because it would absolve the rest of us of guilt) and an American way (there can't be a conspiracy, because then there's no one to take the rap). Mort Sahl went European, all the way into the swamp fevers of the mind of New Orleans District Attorney Jim Garrison.

And the talk shows stopped wanting to hear him go on about the grassy knoll, the two autopsies, the washed-out limousine, Lee Harvey Oswald's marksmanship, Jack Ruby's friends. He wasn't funny. He was also, eventually, unemployed, and bitter, as he made clear in his memoir, *Heartland*. Would he survive? Have any of us?

Even I didn't want to hear at Dangerfield's about the grassy knoll. I wanted to be told that I had survived, which is why I greased the palm of the leader of the goon squad—why do these people always look as if they would stub out their cigarettes in your armpit—and covered and minimumed and hoped.

Although there was a paunch inside the V-necked sweater, he was much, much better than okay. (Yes, I know. Steve Dunleavy in the New York *Post* questioned his taste. Having followed Mr. Dunleavy's coverage of the Son of Sam psychodrama in the *Post*, I don't think he's earned the right to question the taste of Fatty Arbuckle or Joseph Stalin.) Mort Sahl circumnavigated for a splendid hour and a half, to the irritation of the goon squad because the first show ended at midnight when the second show was supposed to begin.

Those stoned munchkins who arrived for the midnight show are one of the little, compelling reasons why I don't usually go to nightclubs. We went home relieved, to listen to old Edith Piaf records, feeling rather as though Norman Mailer—another hero of mine—had managed not to embarrass himself in public. You see, we said to the sleeping children, it takes more than history to kill us off.

Although I wonder as I type: after the monologues of Molly Bloom and Johnny Carson, of Portnoy and Sahl, will we ever be able to think straight again? Not narrow, but straight? No.

Among the Poets

The phone rings at six o'clock in the morning. It is a nice woman telling us that school is closed today on account of the blizzard. I have missed the blizzard. I am information-deprived. I go to the window. Sure enough: New York has been made innocent. Because of the snow, there will be no newspaper delivery, which means that I will not be able to read about the snow, or about what to eat in the snow, or about who went to which snow party wearing what pair of arctic boots and Ultrasuede parka. It will be a long morning.

I turn on the radio to hear about the snow. According to the radio, it continues to snow. This seems to be true. What a comfort that there is something on which everybody can agree. If, last night, I had listened to the radio or watched television, I would have been warned in advance of the blizzard. What a vexation not to have known that New York was being made innocent. Clearly, the woman on the telephone at six o'clock was a superior person, in command of the facts. I am at a disadvantage.

It occurs to me that I almost never listen to the radio, and seldom watch television anymore. I am dangerously ignorant of the latest facts. I am not up to the minute. What was the last time I watched television? Of course: I watched the Super Bowl. I have watched every Super Bowl. Every Super Sunday I have given a party in front of the television set, even when nobody came. Like the vast majority of Americans, I have no way of knowing whether a football game is actually played on Super Sunday, or whether we are watching a simulation, a studio re-enactment of some primal crime: mere theater. This past Super Sunday people drank more than they usually do; by the end of the event we were rooting for another fumble. But on Super Sundays I am not at a disadvantage. Nobody knows anything before I do.

What was I doing last night instead of listening to the radio or watching television? I was, gulp, reading poetry. I don't know why. This is recent, this unmanliness. The neighbors haven't noticed. I hurl myself, of an evening, on the spike of the subjective, the ice pick. According to Robert Lowell—I happened to be reading Robert Lowell—"Age is the bilge we cannot shake from the mop." And: "No dog knows my smell." These are things I was not told by Walter Cronkite or all-news radio. Knowing them does not seem to give me an advantage. To whom might I telephone at six in the morning, saying, "Listen: *No dog knows my smell.*" What would the cats think?

It is impossible, it is in fact absurd, to listen to the radio while drinking the first cup of coffee in the morning. The eyes are unemployed. They look inward. There is nothing there: no bulletins. I am walking around the living room holding on to my coffee cup as though it were a stirrup on a day that is trying to gallop away from me. I don't know which movies, plays and books I may safely avoid. I don't know the hockey scores, even though I have never wanted to know the hockey scores. And I don't like walking around in the morning, anyway.

It is equally absurd to read poetry while drinking the first cup of coffee in the morning. "I pretend my impatience was concision," says Lowell. And: "If we see a light at the end of the tunnel it's the light of an oncoming train." And: "It's an illusion death or technique can wring the truth from us like water." And: "When the black arrow arrives on the silver tray, the fetus has no past. . . ." Or:

> *Dreams, they've had their vogue,*
> *so alike in their modernist invention,*
> *so dangerously distracted by commonplace,*
> *their literal insistence on the letter,*
> *trivia indistinguishable from tragedy—*

Yes. Like television, or all-news radio. I know people who watch television in the morning with their coffee—usually the *Today* show. Some of these people I have managed to like anyway. It seems to me that the color isn't true on television in the morning; it is as if events during the night had been laundered, and ran together. "Description without significance," says Lowell, "transcribed verbatim by my eye." And:

> *We are poor passing facts,*
> *warned by that to give*
> *each figure in the photograph*
> *his living name.*

This is insupportable. I stand at the window watching the innocence come down in the street. Soon I will have to arm myself with a shovel and clear the steps and sidewalk. Maybe I should give a party so my friends can watch: Join us, please, for Dmitri's first coronary; black tie and Ultrasuede.

No. There is a nibble in my head, a modernist invention. Years ago, in the snows of New Hampshire at Christmas, I was in the company of a famous novelist. We were looking at an apple orchard. A curious thing had happened. There had been in the fall an early frost, freezing a number of apples on the branches of the trees. The apples weren't worth picking, and so stayed there. As winter came, the apples turned black. What we were looking at, then, was black apples on gaunt trees against white snow. Very Japanese, and something like a poem by Robert Lowell. I looked at the famous novelist, and the famous novelist looked at me. He said: "If you don't want to use this in a novel, I want to use this in a novel."

According to my friends, and the reviewers, the world doesn't really need another novel from me. So I gave the black apples and the white snow to the famous novelist. They slowed him down for years. I have waited through several of his novels. He has not been able to contain the black apples and the white snow, the black arrow on the silver tray. I take them back. I see the apples now, on the fire escapes across the street, in the falling innocence. That is all the information I have this morning.

Deductible Me

We met for lunch at one of those midtown French restaurants where the menu is a sneer. My friend was buying. He always buys these days. His gainful employment somehow allows him to deduct me as a business expense. I, on the other hand, can't deduct him. In a more civilized culture, this lack of reciprocity would be insupportable. But we are children of the edge, red of fang and claw, wounded bears with magic plastic in our billfolds. These restaurants are our caves.

It had been six months. He hadn't changed much. Sometimes he wears a beard, and sometimes not, as though the hair on his face were seasonal. We assured each other that we were healthy and wise, that our wives thrived, that our children were dauntless. This was a comfort. Lately the telephone calls seem mostly to be about love gone wrong. And twice in the past year old friends have arrived at my doorstep in the middle of the afternoon, with letters addressed to me. I've had to digest these letters, full of surprise and pain, while my correspondents sat in the kitchen waiting for my response. I like reading a Russian novel, but would prefer not to live there.

However, the two of us were all right. My friend is English and bookish, easily deflected by ideas, and playful. Abstractions are his toy soldiers. I can't imagine that his education will ever end. He is a sort of Johnny Appleseed of the arts and sciences, planting geodesic domes, moving on. It was a relief to find people like him when I came to New York ten years ago. It was a relief, as a matter of fact, to find that I could still make friends, that I hadn't used up all of my friend-making wherewithal in college.

We ate our sneers, which had been hushed up with the usual suspicious sauce. My friend wanted to know why, since I had written an article on embarrassment, I hadn't mentioned his moment of profound embarrassment—his related series, really, of profoundly embarrassing moments. Did I remember? Yes: I wake up at times in the middle of the night remembering, as if the embarrassment had been my own, which is probably why I hadn't written about it. The act that cannot be undone . . .

Well, why not? But it's complicated. We used to work together on a magazine. My friend had cultivated the acquaintance of Professor X, an aged and brilliant European scholar, a specialist on Indochina. The professor's English left everything to be desired, but we needed his knowledge and his thinking. My friend became at once a student and a collaborator. He would run the professor's articles through his typewriter several times, trying to make them intelligible, and then go off to a long lunch with the old man for emendations and additions. He came to be trusted. They conspired at many important essays.

On the threshold of one of these lunches, my friend asked me if he could borrow some cash; he was broke. Then he reconsidered. Professor X had never permitted him to pay for their lunch, no matter who was deductible for whom. In their relationship, teacher and pupil, the teacher picked up the check. My friend understood the dignity—the Old World or even Oriental punctilio —of this arrangement, and honored it. Having dealt for years with carnivorous and bankrupt free-lance writers, he probably even found it refreshing. He went off without my money.

Of course, after dozens of lunches, this had to be the one to end with the professor's announcing that they were no longer a teacher and his pupil; they were colleagues, equals, friends. It was therefore appropriate that each pay for his own lunch. Such moments need cymbals, or at least something porcelain to contain them. Emotions are trying to get through the eye of the needle of etiquette. Reciprocity means approval.

My friend's share of the bill came to nine dollars or so. He was cashless, and this particular restaurant took no magic plastic. With as much dignity as he could muster (which is plenty) he suggested that he write a check to Professor X for nine dollars. Professor X might then have ruined everything by saying "Never mind, I'll take care of it." But Professor X, with as much dignity as my friend, accepted the check.

And of course the check bounced. Inexplicably, a check for nine dollars on an account of more than a thousand dollars bounced. We know that information moves in the night, from computer to computer; we are nodes on this dismal grid. But the terrors of embarrassment—must they move, too, these pimply assassins? I was with my friend when he received the bad news. I had never seen him in a rage before. I had never seen an English rage before.

He acquired density as the features on his face—the mouth, the eyes, the nostrils—got smaller, as if to stopper up any leak of the seething inside. He was slower in his density, which contained the panther's contemplation of a killing pounce. He bunched, and seemed to use up most of the space and time around him, as though he controlled the speed in his own dream. We went to his bank. His whisper had nails in it. They were terrified. A vice-president of the bank wrote a letter of apology to Professor X; the error, of course, had been committed by a computer. People are blameless except at night alone. I now understand the British Empire. As the Russians swaddle their children, the English stiffen their lips. The difference is in the style of the inevitable explosion.

Professor X died shortly thereafter. Who knows whether the act was undone, the account balanced? Certainly not the computer. My friend and I sat remembering over our plates. I saw the waiter approach with cups of coffee. I saw my friend gesticulate. I saw the cups and the saucers and the coffee and the rage end up on floors and people all around us. I was helpless. He controlled the speed of the dream. Listen, I wanted to say, but didn't: That story is about fathers and sons. How many fathers are we going to have in our lives, anyway, to tell us that we made it?

I also didn't offer to pay for my share of the bill. I'm deductible.

A Victim of Surprises

Surprise! It was a birthday party, and we therefore behaved like trombones, and the victim was pleased, and the tears fell like dimes, and I looked at the ceiling, which is where I always look when the spy business takes me to the vital and dangerous Upper West Side of the imperial city. Such high ceilings they have on the Upper West Side, as if to accommodate eagles or bats. And yet the people who live under these high ceilings do not, on the whole, seem bigger than the people who live elsewhere in New York, perhaps because they eat so much Chinese food. Considering the housing shortage, maybe we should partition along the perpendicular, or turn all these old buildings on their ears. Turning them on their ears, of course, would block traffic, and that would be a good thing, too. Traffic frightens the eagles.

One must get a grip on oneself. A radical idea is, in my experience, usually a bad idea, a surprise that backfires. Our dissatisfactions and our fantasies do not synthesize; they explode, after which it is necessary to invent nostalgia, and nostalgia is a waste of time, just as time is crystallized guilt. Consider the brushing of one's teeth. A recent novel argued that if the most efficient way of washing dishes is to use hot water, then the most efficient way of washing one's teeth should be to use hot water, not cold. I was radicalized. I tried it. It was like brushing my teeth with calf's-foot jelly, or eating a Chinese bat.

I was pleased that the victim was pleased by the surprise birthday party. In my experience, surprises are as dangerous as birthdays, radical ideas and the Upper West Side. The sort of person who likes a surprise party at his or her expense is also the sort of person likely to have guessed or expected that one was in the works, whereas the sort of person who is genuinely surprised by a party, like a bomb, will probably fear it, or hate birthdays, or get nosebleeds from high ceilings. This is a no-win proposition. Either way, birthdays are taken too seriously. They must bear the weight of our significance, because we can't.

I refuse to take my birthday seriously. That kind of seriousness is for the insurance companies and the astrologers. Time has passed, and so what? When time isn't crystallized guilt, it is an interminable annelid. An annelid, as you know, is a segmented worm or leech. I prefer to think of myself as an eagle.

On the other wing, surprises terrify me. I have committed three or four, behaving like a radical instead of a trombone, and each has caused harm to friends and strangers. I expect the same from the surprises of friends and strangers. I am a defensive driver when I have to go out and block traffic. I do not very often break mirrors or hearts, and this is not because I am graceful but because I am careful. I am aware of a clumsiness inside me, a tantrum, love and death. Surprise is a pratfall; I seek stillness, so as not to perturb. I am zippered up and buttoned down; the beast has brushed his teeth with cold water.

How did T'chen put it a thousand years ago? "Ceaselessly spinning in its silk, the stupid silkworm."

Anyway, the victim of the surprise birthday party cried on me; the lapels of my corduroy jacket were wet with dimes. I think of her as Network, as I think of other enduring friends as Bismarck, Uncle Fix-It, Schoolmarm, Oedipus, the Grand Inquisitor and Libidinal Cathexis. Why should Jung monopolize the archetypes? There are many shadows in my cave, with its Upper West Side ceilings. I think of my friend as Network because she knows everybody and keeps track of them. She is a digest, a library, of our novels. I contain several of her secrets, and some others, plus my own. She contains all of my secrets, and those of the rest of the world. I believe that one of the few times she was ever genuinely surprised was when I proved that I was capable of surprising her. But now, as an eagle or a silkworm, I am careful.

My other archetypes should be self-explanatory: forgiveness—according to Otto von Bismarck, "Life has taught me to forgive much, but to seek forgiveness still more"—and expertise and manners and Daddy and sin and sex. But why are these archetypes so often embodied in women? Because women tend to notice more, to be less surprised, to have paid attention. They also tend to cry, either dimes or chicken soup, and crying is a form of sanity. Eagles should try it. Men, instead, have heart attacks and commit surprising homicides.

I went into another room, with another high ceiling, where a nonwoman was saying: "Pornography used to be the vanguard of the polymorphous perverse. Today that vanguard is advertising. Tomorrow it will be Communist China." This was wrong. This was nostalgia. The vanguard of the polymorphous perverse is, unsurprisingly, birthday parties. They contain eagles, bats, calf's-foot jelly, silkworms and archetypes.

Nobody in the other room was perpendicular. I counted the number of trombones who knew my secrets. It was scary. There wasn't a mirror or a heart I could look into. I didn't like my image. No wonder the ceilings are high. There would be no room otherwise for all the guilt to breathe. Blimps of carelessness looked down. History, consisting of nothing but birthdays and surprises and victims, made a crowd, in which I'm clumsy. Passion and caprice and fairy tales and archetypes . . . enough failures of character to staff a riot . . . radical nostalgia . . . the ultimate tantrum— Friends are our ceilings.

While the Grand Inquisitor wasn't looking, I went home, to the East Side, with my Libidinal Cathexis.

Spinoza and Pork Chops

He was down again among the children, in the libidinal compost heap, thinking about the pork chop problem. The pork chop problem has been described before in this space. It is not the problem of who, on being told to do so, *buys* the pork chops, or the cornflakes, or the vacuum cleaner bags. Or even who cooks them. It is the problem of who conceives of pork chops or cornflakes as a problem, who imagines the *necessity* of vacuum cleaner bags. At dinnertime, essence precedes existence. This branch of metaphysics, like the ritual sacrifice of virgins, has been dominated traditionally by women. But not in our brave new world. In our brave new world, the pork chop problem was his.

He went to the supermarket, a cow paddy of neon and thermoplastic, wherein children caged in grocery carts gave off curdling ululations, and women with bandaged heads licked trading stamps, and there seeped from Muzak speakers a spayed and interminably complaining waltz. He always felt, in supermarkets, unmanned. (In the delicatessens, one can swagger.) If, as he had believed ever since he was old enough to vote, it was somehow unmanly to eat ice cream out of cones on the street—somehow sexually neutral, polymorphous perverse, an affront to the genital organization of the normal American male—then just think how dangerous supermarkets had to be, as though the entire world were an ice-cream cone, a crooning, a form of hypnosis, a controlled environment, a Disneyland. In every Disneyland, he was convinced, while the conscripts were made stupid by a deluge of meaningless choices, while they wheeled their way to a brute accounting, while all this nonsense was going on, Hitler ate the sleeping princess. To push a cart was to push a void, like a kangaroo with an empty pouch or vacuum cleaner bag.

Still, he could go to the supermarket and behave like a kangaroo if his children could go to school, piled down like camels. And they did go to school, every morning of the week rising before dawn to feed the cat and lose a hairbrush and gnaw on a pork chop and fill up their backpacks before hitting the street as the sun did, sidewise, turning the roofs of the neighborhood into a kind of Leningrad, an arctic Italy. It was possible, standing helpless in the living room, to watch their retreat down the street in the reflections on the glass over the two Chinese prints, as if, off to their appointments with geometry and history, they moved between time zones and empires, like motes in the eye of the camel.

He thought: How brave they are, how uncomplaining, in a world they never asked for. Treacherous books and suspect generalizations await them. He admired the braces on their teeth, the trim on their sneakers, their sense of duty. If he would die for them, he could certainly go to a supermarket.

But first, another cup of coffee. According to the radio, letting him in on an interview that had just been published in the Miami *Herald*, Meyer Lansky was willing to tell the world that Meyer Lansky was reading Spinoza. Such news didn't make it any easier to go to a supermarket. Organized crime meets the philosopher of moral autonomy. The maker of license plates sits down with the grinder of lenses. This was precisely the sort of discrepancy about which he liked to lecture his children. He would, of course, have to explain to them who Meyer Lansky was. And then who Spinoza was. He would have to explain too much. Instead, he brooded.

His children were booked up for the afternoon as well: play rehearsals and music lessons and soccer and the dentist. How is it that middle-class children survive all the improvement we foist on them? Meyer Lansky probably knows. There is too much control in the environment. Psychoanalysis would not otherwise be necessary, much less advisable. Why wasn't Meyer Lansky reading Freud?

After his children came back from their afternoon and he came back from the supermarket, there was the usual argument about music on the phonograph. As usual, there was a compromise. He would give up *The Marriage of Figaro* if they would give up

"Red China and the Single Girl." They agreed to Cryer and Ford. Popular music is cheaper than psychoanalysis, or braces.

All right. He solved the pork chop problem with pork chops, cucumbers and hot buttered popcorn. Pork chops are slightly cheaper than sacrificed virgins, as every mother knows. At the dinner table they talked about Spinoza. Rather, he talked, and his children tried to harmonize the expressions on their faces with whatever gust of emotion he seemed to be blowing at any particular moment.

But after dinner, after homework, they played blackjack. And as they were playing blackjack, his son explained that his math teacher was disappointed in trees. Trees, it seems, start out popping off their leaves in a pure mathematical progression, but at some point stabilize and so sully the logic of the theorem. Father was amazed.

So that's what the trees do out there, said the father of his children: sully logic; mess up pure math. I always wondered. Trees are sneaky. When you look at them, they don't seem to be doing much at all. They stand around pretending to be deciduous. But what are the branches really thinking? And at night—unspeakable. Never trust a tree. Keep your windows locked.

His children began to laugh. It doesn't take much, with children, to get a giggle rolling downhill toward the incapacitating guffaw. He went on fantasizing about palm fronds, woodpeckers, Spanish moss, elm disease, tree sex. His children laughed themselves to sleep.

Late that night, grinding his lens, he found two things perfectly clear. First: trees aren't supermarkets or controlled environments, although it is possible to imagine Spinoza out there at night determining the cause of the fall of the pork chops into the empty pouches of the kangaroos. Second: he was probably a better father when he wasn't trying so hard to be one.

To Dance or Not to Dance

My sidekick is transferring names and numbers from an old, broken-down telephone book to a new, squeaky-clean telephone book. I am not. I am on top of the orgone box, sucking cyanide from a peach pit, reading the Egyptian Book of the Dead. It is clear to me this weekend that the sixties are dead. Their license has expired. Back to back, Bella Abzug and Muhammad Ali went down to defeat. I am considering the ontological consequences of this fact. Perhaps we should remove the sixties from our telephone book.

According to my sidekick, we will not, for the time being, remove the name of a psychiatrist of her acquaintance from our telephone book. Why is this? Psychiatry, I explain, is a fifties category—brains washed while you wait, symbolic parricide, the whole syzygy. True man, I point out, has no condition but himself.

Besides, haven't we a viable relationship? That is, she relates to me and I relate to her and neither of us relates to John Travolta. That the sixties should have died giving birth to John Travolta is probably H. R. Haldeman's fault.

My sidekick is firm. She will not remove the name of the psychiatrist from the telephone book until she can bring herself to appear in public on a dance floor. Only then will she consider herself to be a healthy, functioning adult.

I grok that I must be careful. As Valéry observed, "Every word is a bottomless pit." There was, in the mountains last summer, an incident. One night in one of those joints that specialize in loud music and low-calorie beer, out on a toot with the extended family, my sidekick refused to go onto the floor to dance with me or anybody else. She does not believe herself to be an adequate dancer. She did not intend to embarrass herself in front of friends and strangers. And later she was furious at her own behavior.

This lapse from sociability didn't bother me at the time. For one thing, I dance like an oil rig myself, all elbows and pumping action. For another, Ginger Rogers never lit my Bunsen burner. (Cyd Charisse is a separate story.) For a third, if my sidekick were perfect, she wouldn't need me. My many imperfections would offend her. I thought we had agreed to regard each other as Navajo rugs: the occasional flaw was a signature, saying that we were made by hand and not by a machine.

Just because I wasn't bothered, though, doesn't mean the matter wasn't serious. I do not monopolize the available seriousness, a one-man Oberammergau. Other people's seriousness can be cabalistic, druidical, Republican, Spinks-like, dangerous. They, too, have cuds to chew. My sidekick has been brooding for months about a smudge on her self-esteem.

My job, of course, is to fix it up, make it right. I put the Book of the Dead in the refrigerator. I give her some coffee beans to play with. Listen, I say, I went, just like every other stumblebum, to all those dances in all those fetid high school gyms where, after practicing with our mothers, we were supposed in our stocking feet to do the hop. I waltzed in broken boxes. Wherever I stepped, I seemed to break the wing of a defenseless bird. Even the varsity letter sewn to my jacket was a lie; I was a track manager, a clerk of sweat.

And in college, there were mixers. Half boy, half dysthymic stork, I cluttered and sulked and went back to my cell to count, as if they were rosary beads, my pimples, and read *Tonio/Kröger*, which, although I missed the main point, made it perfectly clear that the athlete who could dance would always get the girl and that the artist who lost her would after years and years and years still feel rotten about it; and as bitter time ran out on my club-footed youth I thought: Can you imagine Kafka or Nabokov doing the frug? Or Stephen Dedalus? Or Freud's wolfman? Or Handel's Messiah? Or Kant's categorical imperative? Or the Elgin marbles and the general theory of relativity?

My sidekick admits that she cannot imagine any of this.

And so—I go on, gathering confidence—I was, like you, a child of the fifties. But I cherished my reaction formations and my hostilities, my estrangement and *Gestimmtheit*. Repress, regress:

I would indulge the syn of my own drome. Let them tickle and writhe and square a polka and quadrille for oil and *danse macabre*. I was autonomous, and therefore I could take myself seriously.

Then came the sixties. In a series of seedy discothèques, to which I went only in the company of Erving Goffman and other dramaturgists, I found that people were dancing without looking at one another. It was possible to make a fool of oneself and be unnoticed. Narcissism was liberating. Energy did not require talent; it was self-authenticating. To be sure, a partner or two complained that a key was needed to unlock my knees, that I lacked *soul*—but I have always believed, with Descartes, that my soul, if I have one, is in my pineal gland, not in my pelvis or anywhere else south of the tropic of my bellybutton. I could dance, while at the same time maintaining my autonomy, the *crux criticorum*.

The point—I tell my almost perfect sidekick—is that after the Norman O. Browning of the sixties, nobody cares anymore what any of us do on the dance floors of seedy discothèques or in the privacy of our own refrigerators. Everybody surfs, and nobody watches.

She has, with the coffee beans, fashioned a syzygy that looks like a noose. Listen, she says, her freckles flaring: Has it ever occurred to the Elgin marbles or the categorical imperative that I might want to be better at something than you are?

Well, no, this hadn't occurred to me. Maybe I missed the point of the sixties after all.

The Permanent Relationship

It is Sunday morning. I have emerged from the newspaper and climbed the stairs. The living room, mysteriously, is finished, except for one blank wall. We are waiting to be surprised by a work of art. We have no idea what this work of art will look like, but it is somewhere, in a bin or a loft or a dream, and it will pounce. The blank wall knows. The art will be sincere.

Still, the living room, after months of tinkering, is finished. That was clear last night, when the people and the plants and the books and the music got along. According to the lamp, the lamp had always been there, and couldn't imagine a better place to be. The hole in the wall that pretends to be a fireplace was also sincere, although not as pious as St. John, from the Book of Kells, looking down on the tongue-colored carpet. There was no cockatoo upon the carpet.

I mention cockatoos because I have walked into a poem. Sunlight launders the living room. My best friend is on the couch. She has been eating an orange; sections of peel are on a plate beside her. The day, of course, "is like wide water, without sound / Stilled for the passing of her dreaming feet . . ." The poem, of course, is by Wallace Stevens. It was everybody's favorite poem back in the Pleistocene epoch when I was a college freshman and sincere.

Dreaming feet? I am immediately suspicious. She is manipulating my emotions. To be sure, in the living room there aren't any cockatoos or swallows or pigeons. Because of the cats. Nor is there an insipid lute, although the music stand could use one. St. John is in need of a sepulcher. And my best friend isn't wearing exactly what you'd call a peignoir. She is wearing, in fact, the sort of coveralls one associates with a garage mechanic. But it is dangerous to ignore an orange on Sunday morning. What "large-mannered motions are in her mythy" mind? What "gusty emotions on wet roads on autumn nights? Does ripe fruit never fall?"

I feed the plants and mist the cats. "Death is the mother of beauty," I observe.

"Kiss the dew on my dreaming feet," my best friend replies.

"Supple and turbulent," I look out the window. The "trees are serafim." The sanitation trucks haven't picked up any of the black plastic garbage sacks in three weeks. "Deer walk upon our mountains," I point out, "and the quail whistle about us their spontaneous cries." St. John seems to agree with me. I try again: "You are the 'odor' of my 'plum,'" I tell her.

"Go 'pick the strings of' your 'insipid lute,'" she says. She "undulates ambiguously." She isn't thinking about "tombs in Palestine" or "pears on river-banks" or "the holy hush of ancient sacrifice." She is, instead, reading Trotsky. And she has hurt my feelings.

"Have I hurt your feelings?" she asks. "Do you feel 'the dark encroachment of an old catastrophe'? "

"That's all right," I lie.

"Listen," she says, "according to Edmund Wilson, when Trotsky got to London, Krupskaya met him at the door and said: 'Peró has arrived!' 'Peró' means pen. Now, according to Harrison Salisbury, when Trotsky got to London, Krupskaya met him at the door, took him in to Lenin and Lenin said: 'The Peró has arrived!' Both Edmund Wilson and Harrison Salisbury agree that Lenin was in bed at the time. And both of them cite Trotsky's autobiography as their source. I'm reading Trotsky's autobiography. According to Trotsky, both Krupskaya and Lenin 'had been waiting for me. I was greeted with: "The Peró has arrived."' You see, Trotsky doesn't make it clear which one told him he had arrived."

"So what?" I complain. She is going to Russia soon, and I am not. "What have Edmund Wilson, Harrison Salisbury and Leon Trotsky got to do with *us*, with our permanent relationship?"

"About as much as Wallace Stevens does," my best friend tells me. "I wish the historians would get their act together."

"They will get it straight one day at the Sorbonne," I say. "We shall return from the lecture / Pleased that the irrational is rational."

"Wrong poem."

"Listen, oh you who 'makes the willow shiver in the sun,' two people who have committed themselves to a permanent relationship are supposed to communicate to each other, even if one of them is going to Russia and the other is not. Otherwise, we will end up like our friends."

"Which friends?"

"The women who were here last night in our mysteriously finished living room, drinking our brandy and complaining about men."

"The women who were here last night," says my best friend, "were complaining that the men in their life keep telling them that they, the men, aren't ready yet to commit themselves to a permanent relationship. Certainly that's communication. Everybody is always communicating, especially to psychiatrists, about not being ready yet to commit themselves to permanent relationships. It's just that nobody relates permanently except us."

"Do you mean," I ask, "that communication is not the mother of relationship?"

"I mean," she replies, "that when a man tells a woman that he isn't ready yet for a permanent relationship, he is communicating. What he is communicating is that he doesn't love her enough."

I look at the blank wall of our mysterious living room. I see now the art of this wall, its surprise. It is a picture of complacency. I reach out to my best friend.

She says: "The Peró has arrived!"

Civility

When the news came last week that the English novelist Paul Scott had died, I was sorting books. I should have begun sorting my books—categorizing, alphabetizing, in some cases burning—twenty years ago, but I've pretended instead to subscribe to a principle of serendipity. That is, if I didn't know where to find the particular book I wanted, when I went to look I would find a different, better book, a book I hadn't thought of. This principle of serendipity is opposed to the principle of the study of ablations. An ablation is a tumor or diseased organ, removed by surgery. Scientists study ablations, and try to draw conclusions about boring health from the evidence of extravagant disease. (Only in his sickness does man become interesting, said Nietzsche, who ought to have known.) Many people organize and study their books in the same way, pathologically; they know exactly where to go to pull down an inky ablation of modernism or totalitarian politics or erotic poetry.

Foolishness. The books didn't get sorted because of laziness, procrastination and fear. Laziness: sorting takes time. Procrastination: if I have to search for a book—always the wrong one, anyway—I won't have to work. Fear: as I move from furnished room to small apartment to the various houses in my various lives, empty shelves and blank walls make me feel uneasy and unfurnished, transient, naked to my enemies; and so I slap whatever books in whatever holes, for warmth and protection, making a cave and maybe even a maze. Inside such confusion, they'll never find me; I won't be extradited.

But there I was, trying to be a grownup, when the news came, and I stopped sorting. I doubt whether a shelf of books on death —a subdivision under the rubric of sociology or epistemology or occultism or surprise—would have been of much help.

I hardly knew Paul Scott. I'd met him once, at a small dinner party last year to honor his new novel, *Staying On*. I had, though, spent most of the previous summer reading his masterly *Raj Quartet*—two thousand pages on the end of the British imperial presence in India—to prepare for a review of *Staying On*. I had lived for months in his mind. It was a very civilized place to be.

As literary dinner parties go, which is seldom anywhere important, this one was modest. His American publishers had arranged a table at a tedious Indian restaurant. The Beautiful People didn't show up. It was, instead of black tie, warm gin. And Scott was clearly a sick man, sad in body and soul, on his way to teach in Tulsa, Oklahoma. Nevertheless, he roused himself to several wicked anecdotes. Odd how the writer must pay on such occasions with the coin of personality for the attendance of people whose only excuse is that we have admitted his talent.

I have a friend in Tulsa, Oklahoma. The woods are full of English majors. I commended my friend to Scott, who wrote down his name. This friend would telephone two months later to report Scott's hospitalization for inoperable cancer. It is just as well my friend and I couldn't see each other over the telephone: blue eyes are bad at dread. Neither of us know him well; both of us were drunk on his novels. What a peculiar thing to share, as mice in the wainscoting of a great house.

When Albert Camus died in a sports-car crash, another friend of mine banged on the door of a young woman's apartment at three o'clock in the morning: "The conscience of the West is dead!" he wept. He wanted the young woman more than he needed Camus; grief was one of the coins of his personality. Grief, temporarily, worked. Sex is strange.

So, anyway, this time the news was not a surprise. But I have a responsibility, as a machine for fomenting opinions. I need an angle on my own emotions. I was annoyed at Scott for dying so soon after I, like most Americans, discovered him. I missed something else, besides his genius: his civility. He bothered to tell us wicked anecdotes; he bothered to look up my friend in Tulsa; he bothered to understand Tusker in *Staying On*. In pain, he was kind, not noisy. He advertised nothing of himself. He merely wrote fine books.

Now: I remember another civilized writer whom I met only

once. Nine years ago I went to interview James M. Cain. The author of *Double Indemnity* was very old, and holed in up in a small house in Hyattsville, Maryland. He was alone in the house, unless we count the opera music, but still writing, especially letters to the editors of newspapers. He had given up the bottle and weed, and yet for guests there were cigarettes and whiskey and wicked anecdotes about H. L. Mencken, Walter Lippmann, Harold Ross and Hollywood.

After that interview was published, a great metropolitan newspaper asked me to write an obituary for James M. Cain. But he is very much alive, I said. He won't last, they replied. He didn't, as we know. I wrote for the "morgue" in the present tense; let them, when the time comes, make him obsolete. He died some months ago, and I was halfway through reading his obituary before I realized I had written it.

I had asked Cain: "How do you feel about what Hollywood did to your novels?" He had answered: "Hollywood didn't do anything to my novels." He had pointed to his shelves. *"There* are my novels." No black ties and Beautiful People at his funeral.

All right, my angle: we live in a time when most novelists seem to want to be Prometheus or Faust or Parsifal or Ahab or the bloody white whale; where in the head of the novelist, between his ears, behind his eyes, inside the bowl of bone that holds his brain, there runs a filmstrip, a Hollywood epic, at least three hours long, in CinemaScope, with a cast of thousands, including the entire armies of Spain and Yugoslavia, plus Eva Perón. The exacerbated and imperial self of the writer, his own history and myth and erogenous zones, the fire alarms in his brain circuitry and the symphony orchestra of his singing bones are obligatory and sufficient, on television or elsewhere. The personality is an ablation.

Serendipity led me to Paul Scott and James M. Cain. I will arrange my books according to their civility. Nobody can touch them—these strangers, my friends.

Downwardly Mobile

The following "Letter From the Vicinity of My Inferiority Complex" arrived in this office just in time to comment on the new spring fashions in clothing for men:

You will find me in the denim, where it is rumpled and warm. I am hiding from the polyesters. No iron knows my name, although a couple of leisure suits have been looking for me ever since I publicly disdained triacetate at Bloomingdale's on a Saturday morning before anybody had a chance to pick up anybody else. Three morphodites in flame rayon crepe de chine needed a fourth for sex. They haven't forgiven me yet. But that's another story.

I know that I'm too old for denim. Next year I will be forty, which is obsolete. Vladimir Nabokov pointed out that "the future is but the obsolete in reverse," but you never saw Vladimir Nabokov in blue jeans. In Paris, in blue jeans, pretending to be young, I was heckled by hoodlets wearing tissue-sheer charmeuse and female reindeer antlers. They knew I didn't belong.

And that's the problem. I've never been young and I've never belonged. Neither was allowed in southern California, where I was cloned. Nor were blue jeans. They didn't look upwardly mobile enough. Our mission, and all of us chose to accept it, was to get out of the lower middle class and into graduate school before the Pentagon could send us to Southeast Asia where the Vietcong wore two-ply mercerized cotton and imperial silk pajamas.

It should have been possible, in southern California, to figure out appropriate attire for the various social occasions, once I'd burned my knickers. But I was always a little off, a step behind or to the side. Thus, I wore for basketball games what should have gone bowling: shantung jacket with Aztec eagles and serpents embroidered on the back, purple stretch pants, bone-colored suède leather shoes. I wore for beach parties and grunion hunts what should have gone to the senior prom: pearl-buttoned whipcord ranch jacket, khaki jodhpurs, espadrilles. I wore for miniature golf that which should have been reserved for drive-in restaurants and hubcap stealing: pavé-mirrored motorcycle jacket, celery-colored hiphuggers, white vinyl crash helmet, alligator lift shoes with spring-action tongues. At commencement, when my peers showed up in towel shirts, Bermuda shorts and brandy-tinted vamp-strapped beach-bunny sandals, there I was in skullcap, chasuble and buskins.

What a relief it was to go away to college, far from the anarchy of southern California, the mysteries of desert style. No more string ties, mandarin collars, fundoshis, rebozos, striped Arabian jump suits, plum-colored calypso pants, *peau de soie* sweat shirts and graffiti-speckled leotards. I was initiated into the securities of charcoal gray, olive drab and brown tweed, plus elbow patches. I could tell by looking in the mirror that I no longer belonged to the lower middle class. I would wear such clothes until they, and I, rotted, until the buttons fell off my collars and my bones stopped singing.

The 1960's, as we're all tired of hearing, messed up everything. A Cultural Revolution mandated that men look like pimps or paratroopers or Che Guevara or a distempered raccoon. At the great metropolitan newspaper for which I type, there was resistance to this commercialization of the libido, these gaudy advertisements for an inauthentic self. But as the seasons went by, I am sorry to say, that resistance crumbled. You would walk into an elevator and find yourself staring at a tie the size of a diaper—looking, in fact, as if it had been used first as a diaper, or hanging out there in the middle of the olive drab like a tongue with elephantiasis. Sports jackets straight off a linoleum rack in surprising Queens soon followed. Finally, neon pants.

I tried to get with it. I am never with it. It leaves without me. I bought a suit I thought had flair. The first time I wore it in the elevator, a man said to me: "What did you do, shoot a mattress?" He had what I suppose is the layered look. That is, he looked like a garage sale. I examined my fellow passengers. It was impossible to tell who did, and who didn't, belong to the lower middle class. Then what was the point?

I sit at the window thinking about the point. The streets teem with men exhausted before they can even get to work. Why are they exhausted? Because they have used up their decision-making wherewithal before breakfast. First they have to decide which parts of their heads to shave or fertilize, blow or spray. Then they must decide what they want to smell like: leather, or trees, or Mannlicher-Carcano BB guns, or the guts of a sperm whale. After that, what do they want to look like? Color combinations are bewilderingly multiple: ice blue, pink blush, lemon cream, sagebrush green, banana, bamboo, crocus, fawn, terra cotta, mulberry, jellybean, oatmeal and so on. But color combinations are easy compared to the image, the persona, the *me* of the morning. Do they choose to impersonate a Russian peasant, a Greek fisherman, a Marseilles sailor, an Apache Indian, a Hebrew prophet or a mortician?

I am not any of these people, and even if I had the energy to try to pretend to be one, I know I wouldn't pass. I would be found out, as somehow they always seemed to know in southern California. It occurs to me: from among the many sorts of failure, each man unerringly selects the one that will most compromise his self-respect.

And so I have switched to blue jeans and checkered denim shirts. Oh, I have a turtleneck for blizzards and, because people die and get married, I will go as far as corduroy for formal occasions. But I will go no further. Let them, in their banditti blouses and their chaps and their tarbooshes and their huaraches, hoot. I belong to myself, downwardly mobile, the child I never was.

Pregnant

Is parturition contagious? He is on the living-room floor again, listening to the house be empty. Part of his family has gone, and part has yet to arrive. In two hours he will go to the airport. He spends more time in airports than he does in bathrooms. He occasionally feels like an airport; the announcements over his public-address system are in Twi or Tagalog. He ought to be thinking about the weekend, because the weekend will require all his cunning. He is thinking instead about parturition, because everybody seems to be pregnant.

How has this happened? Well, he more or less grasps the primitive part: the clumsy dialectic of man and woman. But *why*, when it has been generally agreed at the High Table of the *Zeitgeist* that children are inconvenient? Children reduce the number of weekends we can go skiing. A resolution against children has been approved at the subcommittee meetings of the various liberation groups. Soon we will be so liberated that there will be nobody left for the Sullivanians to analyze; everybody will be skiing. Oedipus stops here.

But people keep on doing it, getting married and getting pregnant and telling other people about it without the slightest trace of embarrassment or apology. One pair of friends already knows the sex of the child it will have in July. Another pair will wait until August to find out. On the Lexington Avenue subway just the other snowstorm, he was poked in the stomach by an old friend who removed from her purse an envelope that contained a photograph of her baby, in her womb, taken that very morning. This baby, too, was waiting for August.

He isn't sure he approves of know-it-all medical science. But he has clearly spotted a trend. Two out of these three fathers-in-waiting will be more than sixty-five years old by the time their new children finish college, which is a little late for skiing. All three expectant mothers are working women, managers of their own talent. All six parents-to-be are undismayed. On the contrary, they are pleased to the point of gloating. Their glee is almost smug. They must not have spoken recently to Gore Vidal.

He prefers contemplating parturition to contemplating Yasir Arafat, Cambodia, the kidnapping of Italians or the vote in Albany on capital punishment. He has been a father, not a killer, for sixteen years. The son he will meet at the airport now shaves twice a month whether he wants to or not. There is no longer any way of preventing his daughter from becoming a teen-ager. His responsibility on the weekend, in fact, will be to superintend the birthday party acknowledging that his daughter is twelve.

Once more, then, beef fondue, Bingo, bowling, the ululations of the rock *Zeitgeist* and a swamp of sleeping bags on the top floor. The girls—and they *are* girls, not little people tragically oppressed by the sexism of the English language—will babble through the watches of the clockless night about boys (who may or may not metastasize into Arafats). The older brother will be hiding out in the cellar to read Pliny the Elder in the original. The father will pretend, while dismantling the popcorn machine in the kitchen, that he is puissant.

The father puts Franz Lehár on the phonograph: *Die Lustige Witwe*. The father is corny. He thinks of disposable diapers, sprained ankles, strained carrots, the alphabet, concussions, swimming lessons, shoes, gerbils, ketchup, toilet training, firecrackers, boats, teeth, cartoons, babysitters, the New Math and the old verities, basketball, chemistry, mumps, questions. What an airport, or a hospital, or a school! Gates and beds and desks, and dreams impossibly quaint or as vainglorious as a sword. Mittens and boots and betrayals and valentines. Too much salt and television. Ingratiating swagger. A quite astonishing capacity for forgiveness.

He has found lately that, in the clutches of music, he fantasizes on a domestic scale. He no longer bothers to imagine his rescuing of his helpless children from the thugs of the world. In his day-dreams, the children are competent. His daughter sings, his son is on the clarinet and their father plays the piano. This is preposterous, because their father plays the piano about as well as he solves quadratic equations. He doesn't even have a piano; his equations are triangular and his quantity, alas, is very well known and of low power.

But he persists, as though a typewriter were a piano, in pretending that a happy beginning and middle and end are in his power to confer. They warble, and there is surprised applause. Waiters in his imaginary nightclub weep into the pisco sours of television producers who are so transported that they decide Donny and Marie have overbite. The Mafia tries to muscle in. Father destroys the ozone layer of the Mafia with the aerosol can of his charm, not to mention too many belts of judo.

No. For his children he wishes a world without kidnappers, Arafats, Cambodia and the electric chair. For his friends, he wishes children, brave and competent and festering with questions. For the *Zeitgeist*, and the subcommittees on selfishness, and the liberated thugs, he wishes a permanent moratorium: concussions and mumps. His friends are affirmative and puissant; they belly-flop into the future; they wing it. We will endure, he thinks, if we listen to the corny music. We will prevail, he hopes, if there is glee in our blood and joy in our sleeping bags and fondue for our chromosomes . . . and if we believe that our children—our modifications and our enhancements and, ultimately, our teachers —are more important than skiing and murder.

It is time to go to the airport. Our flight has not been canceled.

The Burning Question

It is a tradition. Every year at my daughter's birthday party, somebody gets burned by the boiling vegetable oil that seems to be necessary in order to achieve the charred chunks of beef we are fondueing. This is tolerable if the victim is a child, because children ought to be burned if they insist on waving their fondue forks around in the air, and stabbing one another, like a gaggle of glue-sniffing pirates. This is not, however, tolerable if the victim is a father. But I am getting ahead of myself, and I'm too tired to keep up.

They say that men can't cope. They lie. Men can cope; it just takes men much longer, and many more steps, to do so. It is amazing that women go away, to Russia or Cygnus X-1, as if they were independent human beings with free will and credit cards and desires and dreams of their own. They leave, especially on the day before a birthday party. And they weren't much use the previous week, either, always thinking about themselves instead of the men in their family.

I apologize to the mothers of the friends of my daughter. These mothers had a perfect right to ask questions when a strange man called them on the telephone, demanding that their daughters come to my house on a Saturday night with sleeping bags.

On the other hand, only one of my daughter's friends showed up with a sleeping bag. I don't know what the others slept in. Maybe the bedroom curtains. I didn't inquire. I was busy fixing the leak in the sodium pump in my brain.

It would have been possible, on one brave shopping expedition, to secure the necessities: the hacked-up beef, the mangy carrots, the fierce cake, soda pop of sufficient moxie to rot the enamel off all teeth, bags of whatever has been done recently to innocent potatoes, cheap and gaudy prizes for deplorable contests, allergy pills for those who sneeze upon seizing a cat that's been trying to hide, a new sodium pump, a mature woman.

But, like many men, I am methodical. I do one thing at a time. (This, a form of monogamy, is not to be disparaged.) First I bought Scotch. The rest took four hours and seven miles.

Also, like many men, I am forever being surprised at what isn't there, what has inexplicably run out: vegetable oil, liquid Sterno, charm, courage and my wife. Liquid Sterno proved as difficult to find as any recent newspaper stories about *The New York Times* search for the Loch Ness monster. And it came in the form of a can of what looked like gelatin. I poked holes in the gelatin in a vain attempt to liquefy it. Consequently, it resembled a cache of blue eggs abandoned by a heartless grunion.

I see that I haven't explained that liquid Sterno is necessary to maintain a flame under the bowl of our fondue pot, which hails from overrated Scandinavia. Thus, after you have burned yourself bringing the vegetable oil to a boil on the stove, you need somehow to ignite a pile of gelatinous eggs and think about Ingmar Bergman.

The first of my daughter's friends arrived at exactly the moment I discovered that four fondue forks were missing. Plastic spoons were no substitute. Neither was a Civil War cavalry sword. Why does none of this ever happen to Mimi Sheraton or Nika Hazelton or Rose Franzblau or Max Lerner or David Niven or Ingmar Bergman?

The treasure hunt ended at exactly the moment the boiling vegetable oil spat at me. Whereas children are traditionally burned on the hands, I was burned on the lips. I'd rather not discuss it. I applied a poultice of bedroom curtain soaked in Scotch.

On the one hand, nobody complained about the fact that I had forgotten to make any fancy sauces—idea of apricot, fixation of cashew, animus of huckleberry—to go along with the fondue. They ignored, in fact the ketchup, the mustard, the mayonnaise and my blistered lips.

On the other hand, nobody ate her carrots.

Why, I wonder, did my wife take the fondue forks with her to Russia, where nobody eats anything but cabbage and words?

Bingo was so boring that the twelve-year-olds started telling twelve-year-old jokes. Rock music was inevitable.

It occurred to me in the kitchen, as my daughter and her friends were dismantling the top floor of this miserable house, that I had made an error in not going out into the neighborhood one last time to purchase paper plates and plastic cups. The purpose of paper plates and plastic cups is to avoid dishes. I do not think of myself as a cafeteria. If I had been burned on the hand, I would have a medical excuse for not washing the dishes.

Unfortunately, my daughter and her friends are clever and, one must admit, talented. They had decided to put on a show. Putting on a show required noise, feet, endangered plants and an audience. My consciousness having been raised so high that I can't see anything that isn't suspicious, I thought it was a bad idea for six twelve-year-old girls to perform in a living room for a man with blistered lips. Why weren't they watching television, or washing dishes, instead?

But, of course, I sat down on the coffee table to watch. And the coffee table collapsed. I mean, I broke the coffee table. Cans of enamel-rotting soda pop, shards of tortured potato, cheap and gaudy cats, my self-esteem and my composure and my ashtray all spilled onto the living-room rug. I looked at the ashtrays. They seemed to me ears in which someone, perhaps Ingmar Bergman, had stubbed out the points of a burning question.

It was I who was questionable.

At exactly that moment, I decided three things: (1) I was going to bed; (2) I intended overnight to grow a mustache to obscure the blisters on my lips and to punish the women in my life, and (3) I had to get up at dawn because I'd forgotten that all these pimples would want to eat breakfast.

The Ear

He used to be less of an ear. He used to be more of a mouth. When he wasn't talking, he was thinking about what he would say next. It is not very interesting, being a mouth. He had never learned anything with his mouth open, except what his feet tasted like. It is, in fact, difficult to *see* with your mouth open, which is why people who read while moving their lips take such a long time to finish a book.

Where were we? Yes. As St. John Baptist de la Salle pointed out in *The Rules of Christian Manners and Civility* (1695), "The ears should be kept perfectly clean; but it must never be done in company. It should never be done with a pin, and still less with the fingers, but always with an ear-picker." Or a washrag. Or a Popsicle stick.

His used, bruised ear throbs in the night. He has recently gone through a couple of weeks of hard listening. Alternatives weren't viable. Everybody in his immediate neighborhood had just arrived from somewhere else exotic—from San Diego or Ithaca or Gainesville or Jerusalem or Moscow. They swelled with oral epics. They opened their suitcases and their mouths. Out came wooden eggs, tins of caviar, lacquered boxes, Bedouin deodorant beads, Red Army belts, tea cozies in the guise of peasant dolls, antique kohl holders in the shape of peacocks, books on icons, Lenin lapel pins, kibbutzim honey, buffalo-grass vodka, anecdotes, diseases.

How could he talk back to, compete with, this overdose of information? Of what compelling interest was his meaningful relationship with his typewriter, or the appearance of the brave crocuses in the garden, or the broken doorbell, or the cost of living index?

He listened and listened. His entire body was an ear, a drum they danced on. Of course they needed to babble, to be debriefed. They had swallowed cultures whole; or, perhaps more dangerously, had dissipated the gas of themselves in the vast spaces of the historical drama, and were feeling attenuated, incoherent. They had to reassemble, to congeal, around objective fact.

About those Bedouin deodorant beads, for instance. They were strings of cloves. You wet them and then went out into the hot desert air. As the water evaporated, you began smelling like a clove. He wasn't sure he could use this information, and any information that can't be used is un-American.

On the other hand, he was pleased to learn that Israel supplies, by plane, the best fresh flowers to be found in Western Europe. He liked the idea of planeloads of freshly cut flowers leaving daily from the Holy Land. Imagine the export not of oil or transistor radios or rhetoric or terror but flowers.

On the third hand, he was depressed to hear that there was a revolving door in the Hotel Europeiskaya in Leningrad. Back in the days when he had been a mouth instead of an ear, he had gone to the Soviet Union and hadn't found any revolving doors. This meant that Russians had to spend a good part of every winter day hacking their way in and out of public buildings as if trying to escape a disabled submarine through a single torpedo tube. Perhaps the Russians hadn't yet invented the revolving door. That seemed inconceivable. Revolving doors must have occurred to Peter the Great, who was one.

He had spent a great deal of time thinking and talking about the Russian revolving-door problem. Since everything else that didn't work in the Soviet Union had been blamed on the Germans, he had finally decided that the Germans during World War II deliberately destroyed all the revolving doors in Russia. Knowing the Germans, they probably had a special anti-revolving-door gun, the *Gegendrehtürartilleriegeschütz*. To be told now that there was a revolving door in one of the oldest hotels in Leningrad was to be injured in the objective fact, to be diminished in the fancy and to lose a cherished anecdote.

But he is listening to the vital organs of the house. In various rooms this thick and fidgety night, various mouths are in and out of various beds. The breaking of dishes and the flushing of toilets tell tales of dislocation. Their time is out of joint. So, too, are their bodies: not yet mended. Sprained brains. They know too much. Where is the ear, the wastepaper basket to contain the wrappers and pits of thoughts and feelings? The ear is hiding. If it is true (and it must be) that big eyes require more sleep, the only ear in the house needs some silence.

He wonders: When did I become an ear? It is, obviously, convenient to have a newspaper in which to put most of your opinions. That way you don't have to bother your friends with your mouth, and a lot of time is left over for listening. But does this mean that the drama has passed him by, or gone through him, on its way to Jerusalem or Moscow, as though he were a revolving door? Will he spend the rest of his life waiting for someone else to bring back a rose of Sharon and a triptych of St. Nicholas, listening to other people talk about their divorces and their jobs?

No. He thinks he was probably shocked into shutting up and trying to be an ear when, first, he realized that his children had interesting things to say, and then, second, he did a number of things he had told himself he would never do, things about which his opinions were irrelevant. So perhaps it was only decent to listen for a while to his friends and children. He is gathering evidence and forming conclusions and examining the details of his feelings. Presently, loudly, he will intervene.

Everybody Is Wrong

About eleven years ago, my penultimate wife and I went to a movie in Boston. It was necessary to go to this movie in order to be able to fend off the people in Cambridge, Massachusetts, who made it their business at social gatherings to spill red wine on you while babbling about movies and group sex. In other words, we went to the movie as if to a nurse for a vaccination against the sin of not being with it. The movie was *Blow-Up*.

I should explain that eleven years ago was a difficult time in my life. Actually, there is a difficult time in my life at least once a month, but this one was especially difficult: I was out of a job. A book on which I had worked very hard had been disdained by almost every publisher on the Atlantic Seaboard. The car I drove was an Edsel. And a great many people in Cambridge, Massachusetts, although they'd deny it now, still thought the war in Vietnam was peachy-keen because, after all, it was being conducted by a bunch of Harvard professors with napalm in their book bags.

Blow-Up was awful. While deploring pop culture, Antonioni ate it up; his camera smacked its lips. Such gaudy complaints about the alienation and sterility of modern tra-la-la aren't even interesting in French novels written by bowls of fruit or airports. I came out of the theater feeling sorry for myself. If Antonioni was serious, I couldn't be. So *that's* what they want, I thought— "they" being, I suppose, the gatekeepers and commissars and lap dogs and Brussels sprouts of the *Zeitgeist*. No wonder my book was unpublished; I was so out of it that I didn't even want to get in.

A depression followed, during which I reread the novels of Evelyn Waugh and shaved with a fork. This depression lifted only with the publication in the *New Republic* of Pauline Kael's review of *Blow-Up*. She was sarcastic, and I aspire to sarcasm because being bittersweet all the time is boring. She was also fierce: "Antonioni loads his atmosphere with so much confused symbolism and such a heavy sense of importance that the viewers use the movie as a Disposall for intellectual refuse." And she asked a pertinent question: "Was there ever a good movie that everybody was talking about?"

I have tried as my arteries have hardened in this imperial city to follow the advice implicit in that question. If everybody is talking about it, don't go. It is easier not to go if you live, as I do now, on the East Side of Manhattan, where most of the chichi movie houses are the size of orthopedic gyms, and you have to stand in a line in the rain for an hour with three hundred hairdressers and Palestinian refugees, being barked at by a hoodlet in a Mussolini carhop uniform, only to find there is no buttered popcorn because if you munch in the thrall of Cinema Art you aren't serious and might, besides, stain your toga.

I am an American, even if I would prefer not to drive an Edsel or any other car. I insist on buttered popcorn when I go to the movies, and on hot dogs when I go to a ball game, and, for the sake of variety, at least once a month, the missionary position when I go to bed.

But an American simply can't not go to a movie everybody's talking about, if only to practice our disdain. Oddly enough, it was Miss Kael herself who started everybody talking about *Last Tango in Paris*. I spent an enormous amount of money to watch Marlon Brando keep his pants on. I spent just as much money to watch novels I happen to like—by Scott Fitzgerald, Nathanael West and Raymond Chandler—turned into Wagnerian soap opera and finger-painting therapy by directors whose problems with their Gestalt are of no conceivable interest to anyone except their mothers and a few heavy-breathing critics with pencils in their noses. I didn't have to pay to watch *Network* because I was rented to write about it, but when (after two hours of Sidney Lumet's lumpy thwacks and Paddy Chayefsky's self-righteous monologues stuffed like pianos into William Holden's mouth) we finally got to the Arabs (the Arabs, for Allah's sake, on Sixth Avenue!), I demanded a refund anyway.

No, I don't hate movies: One thinks of *Citizen Kane, Casablanca, The Rules of the Game, Jules and Jim, Singin' in the Rain, Persona* and *Smiles of a Summer Night, On the Waterfront* and even *Nashville.* I fell in love with what's-her-name in *The Black Rose* when I was ten years old. My ultimate wife insists on seeing every movie with a nun in it, despite the fact that she's exactly as much a Roman Catholic as Leon Trotsky. It seems, though, that I hate every movie that everybody talks about.

And everybody includes children, who increasingly assume that they have a right to an opinion and my money. These creeps prefer *Saturday Night Fever* to *Annie Hall.* All right: *Star Wars.* (A little comic-book Fascism never hurt anybody but Europe.) And *Close Encounters of the Third Kind.* (I would like to look like François Truffaut instead of, alas, Wally Cox.) But I draw the line, with *Saturday Night Fever,* at gang rape and clichés. Don't tell me about the dancing. Has anybody seen *Singin' in the Rain* or *The Band Wagon* or *Gold Diggers of 1933* or *Calamity Jane?* *Saturday Night Fever* is the proletarian novel mugged by rockers not even brave enough to be punk: amplified lumpen.

Finally, everybody is talking about *An Unmarried Woman.* And Jill Clayburgh is, admittedly, terrific, even though Alan Bates does not exist in the lives of any of the unmarried women I know, and Paul Mazursky looks at the world through the lens of a lollipop, and almost every agony of love and work and parenthood is trivialized in Technicolor—picture postcards from the zone of death, the Winter Palace of the heart—and why can't the movies everybody talks about be bothered or obliged to think? *An Unmarried Woman* is talking about my life, and it is slick and stupid, and a dozen novels every other month are better acquainted with nuance.

Why doesn't everybody, at the next dinner party where white wine or vermouth cassis will be spilled on my book bag, talk about the new novel by Mary Gordon or Jill Robinson or Toni Morrison or Anne Tyler? Because everybody is lazy, and maybe I go to the wrong dinner parties, and when do the Red Sox come to town?

Not Quite

It is now possible to divide the world into two classes of people. There are those who will permit me to make a fool of myself in public, and there are those who won't. This has been a trying week.

For a month I hid in my cave, gnawing on a praline and thinking about the neutron bomb. But every April the book people come out of the woodwork for the National Book Awards, a fertility rite consisting of three days of ceremonies, seminars, tantrums and cirrhosis of the liver, the purpose of which is to cause dismay and confer prizes that are never reported on the front page of *The New York Times*. At the Biltmore, the Americana, Carnegie Hall and the Four Seasons, everybody who has ever been guilty of association with rational comment and abstract ideas seems to show up with a new job and a new sidekick. It is, if you have been in the business a while, like drowning in friends.

I have decided not to discuss the piano in the bar at the Americana, but it almost changed my mind about the neutron bomb.

Anyway, I had to face them, these friends, these anthologies. Face is exactly the word. You see, I have been trying to perpetrate a mustache. What I have managed to achieve so far was variously described last week as hesitant and nauseating.

My children would agree. For some reason it is all right for a fifteen-year-old boy to try to look like Emiliano Zapata or Big Foot, but his father is not allowed to change so much as the frames on his glasses. I am to remain fixed, marooned, in my suckling pig of a face, my innocence, never to find out whether I am even capable of what Thomas Fuller called "ornamental excrement" on the chin or lips. I, who must shave this face every morning for the rest of my life, will never have anything else to look at in the mirror. If you had my face, you would be bored, too.

But I am not here to discuss pianos or children. Children will grow up and go away and forget to write. I am here to thank those writers and editors and critics and paperhangers—a distinct minority—who were gracious enough last week to say "interesting" or "promising" or "well . . ." or who kept their mouths shut, or who didn't notice. I am here to stamp my foot at the real majority, most emphatically including the churl who handed me, wordlessly, a card with the name and telephone number of an exterminator on it. That churl had better not write a novel while I'm in town.

One would have thought that book people would be more charitable. Half of them, after all, look like ashtrays or armpits most of the time. The other half are women who are too young for me. Faulkner and Hemingway had mustaches, not to mention Hitler and Stalin. S. J. Perelman, who was honored last week for "Special Achievement" by the Association of American Publishers, has a mustache. S. J. Perelman was introduced at Carnegie Hall by Gene Shalit. I rest my case.

Why am I growing it? Because it isn't there. Because I need something to write about in this column. (Do you think it's easy to write this column? I wish you the hives. They cut the sex out of this column, and they don't want politics in this column, and my children haven't said anything interesting since Guy Fawkes Day, and I'm not hungry.) Because I am at home alone a lot, where I am obliged to watch the insouciant cats have too much fun rubbing their whiskers on the phonograph records and the quarter-pound of butter. Because if the magnolia bush in the back yard can so mindlessly and affectingly sprout, why can't I? Because I shall require a transplant for the top of my head. Because I like my coffee filtered. Because I need something else to think about besides the neutron bomb. Because my sidekick is ticklish.

One would have thought that book people would be more imaginative and compassionate. In my opinion, and I am the king of this space, the following comments aren't witty: "Your nose is dirty." "Where did you find that caterpillar?" "Have you stapled your toothbrush to your upper lip so you can use it after every drink?" "The S.O.S. magic scouring pad strikes again!"

"Ugh, gross." I get enough of this flapdoodle from the little non-book people whose allowances I have canceled. For my son I wish a sidekick whose braces are as formidable and unalloyed as his own and an electromagnetic wave the size of Moby Dick, so that when she kisses him, they will be locked together at the teeth until their feet fall off and they find it impossible to yawn.

I ask the book people to consider Walt Whitman, Mark Twain, Kurt Vonnegut, Ernie Kovacs and Rasputin.

The problem is my mother, whom I must face sometime this summer at a wedding that is in every other respect desirable. Mothers are notorious for wanting children without hair. I went among the book people to practice, to believe in my mustache, to solicit sympathy and approval. I appreciate being laughed at almost as much as I appreciate soybeans and neutron bombs.

Günter Grass? Dean Acheson? Tom Dewey? Myra Breckinridge?

The worst face to put on this whole problem is to conclude that when men grow hair on our faces it is an admission that, deep down, we have never been sure that we are intrinsically interesting. The best face to put on it is to declare that we are unwilling to admit that we are *finished*.

Almost, though.

California in Rochester

They are very young, my friends. (Everybody all around me gets younger and younger; it is a deplorable trend.) They have lived together in Rochester for several years. Living together in Rochester is somewhat better than living alone in Rochester, but still no bargain. It seems always to be cold in Rochester; in mid-April it was snowing in Rochester; Rochester is the second cloudiest city in America, behind Seattle. In massive, windowless buildings all over Rochester, people are coating film. On the campus of the Rochester Institute of Technology, the art students must trudge a mile over the frozen tundra to achieve a dandy wind tunnel. It is dangerous to cross the frozen tundra with a large canvas; the wind picks you up like a sail and you are suddenly in Buffalo. My colleague Richard Eder suggests that a new school of American miniaturists will emerge, all of them former art students at R.I.T. who had to carry their paintings in their pockets.

Don't ask why Richard Eder was in Rochester. He was on his way to Milwaukee. One of the nice things about reviewing books for a living, instead of reviewing plays, is that books stay home. I was in Rochester to defend the printed word against the apocalyptic seizures of McLuhanism, and to see my young friends. At least Richard Eder had a trench coat. I am writing a memo to God about the weather in Rochester. While I am at it, I will explain that it is the purpose of parking lots to be *near* something. Why are all of Rochester's parking lots in Buffalo?

My young friends are soon to be married, and to leave Rochester. I, of course, consider both of these decisions to be sensible. She was glad to see me because she is my sister, and that is her job. He was glad to see me because my sister is a vegetarian, and I was taking them out to a restaurant where he was allowed to look at meat.

My young friends have a car. It is obligatory in Rochester to have a car, in order to occupy all the space in the parking lots in Buffalo. This car lacked a back seat. There was, instead, a kind of wind tunnel, where my sister stretched out flat, making jokes. I sat in front because I could not stretch out, even on a rack; my body was a clenched fist. We drove through swamps and psychiatric hospitals to their apartment. It consists of two rooms. I don't count the kitchen because young people in the reduced circumstances of graduate studentship don't really have kitchens; they have closets. Besides, without meat there is no kitchen; there are merely ice cubes.

In the smaller of these two rooms, they work. In the larger, they read and listen to music and sleep. They sleep in a loft abutting the nonkitchen, which is an efficient use of space and a fine place to hide the Sunday newspapers, unless you are not a midget and want some ice cubes. I am known occasionally to exaggerate, and my young friends aren't midgets. But neither have they ever been asked to join a basketball team. They are close to the earth, to be nearer, I suppose, to the roots they eat. I thawed.

And I was surprisingly happy. My sister grew up in California, where she learned to play the guitar and sing "All My Trials" and set type and eat roots and stretch out to make jokes. She smiles constantly, which isn't popular in Rochester, where they think you're trying to steal their body heat or the coat on their film. Of Whittaker Chambers, Arthur Koestler said: "Such peculiar birds are found only in the trees of the revolution." Of my sister, I say: "Such a splendid bird can thaw even Rochester." The best sort of Californian makes a California nest, even in the trees of Eastman Kodak. She brought California with her, like a guitar: whitewashed walls, smoky cats, impertinent plants, books, records, prints and sunlight. There was probably sand in the bathroom, although I never found a bathroom. I thawed in California, which is the idea that there is a future.

And I was pitched into the past, remembering a two-room apartment in San Francisco when my circumstances were so reduced that the bed was in a closet and the kitchen was a hot plate and we listened to Harry Belafonte and read Herb Caen. Grim, indeed, but we didn't know it at the time. Children and artichokes and Lee Harvey Oswald were still in the future, unseen ghosts. It was possible to go on a Sunday to Golden State Park, for free, to eat sourdough and drink zinfandel and watch the dentists on their polo ponies brandish mallets. Between one chukker and another we would tread upon the green, and tamp down divots dislodged by the hooves of the rich. Our film had not yet been developed.

The young are brave, of course, because they are innocent and belong in California, where nothing dies, including love. A Rochester is unimaginable to the young. I am, humbly, a miniaturist, with pocket-size thoughts. In Paris, in the Tuileries, the trees are wired for sound. You can listen to a poet, as long as he is French. Poets are the ghosts in the trees of the French Revolution. I don't know about Rochester. Maybe there's a tree in my sister's bathroom, with the sand. Maybe the bathrooms, like the parking lots, are in Buffalo.

I am a tree in a wind tunnel; youth blows by. California recedes from the Union. My sister plays the guitar; her hair is chords. I wish her a future, and love, and someplace to park, and lofty music.

On Honor

Shakespeare asked in *Henry IV:* "What is honour? A word. What is that word honour? Air. A trim reckoning! Who hath it? He that died o' Wednesday. Doth he feel it? No. Doth he hear it? No. 'Tis insensible, then? Yea, to the dead. But will it not live with the living? No. Why? Detraction will not suffer it. Therefore I'll none of it. Honour is a mere scutcheon—and so ends my catechism."

This, certainly, is the modern attitude. Science, on the one hand, informs us that we are peripheral to the real business of the universe, which is probably entropic. Literature, on the other hand, is all fire alarms and anti-heroes. Virtue is considered quaint; we have turned our fig leaves into antimacassars. Only the self abides, and it is a craven thing, a dustbin of appetites, a howl.

What a shock it was, then, to discover just the other week that deep down inside of me, as vestigial as an appendix, as tiny as a guppy or a fingernail, I had a sense of honor, and this sense of honor had been offended. I walked around the block, of course, and spat at cats, but it was still there. It twitched.

"It is gone," said Edmund Burke. "That sensibility of principle, that chastity of honour, which felt a stain like a wound." Burke was writing about the French Revolution. I, as usual, am writing about my craven self. But it isn't gone. A part of me had been offended that I didn't even know I had.

The details are unimportant, and perhaps even unseemly. It should be enough, as background, to say that I have a poison-pen pal, a corporate gnome who takes it upon himself once or twice a year to mail me a black valentine. In my promiscuous opinionizing, I have again outraged him. I am to be chastised with the scorpions of his ungrammatical prose. My intelligence, my discretion and my ancestry will be questioned.

I suspect that anyone in the promiscuous-opinionizing racket has such poison-pen pals. Once we get over our injured feelings— we are, after all, Americans and therefore require the whole world to approve of us—we slouch back to our typewriters. My corporate gnome was not significant. He wasn't even sincere. Invariably, his outrage had to do with a negative evaluation I had filed concerning a project in which he had a substantial financial investment. His letters were typed on a ribbon of money. Carbon or Xerox copies were sent to the principals and other investors in his project, as well as to almost everybody else except the Shah of Iran. Servile flimflam, I told myself with the little duck of my head I affect when rolling with the punch of reality.

And I never responded. It didn't seem dignified to respond. Responding to repeated animadversions on my brainpower and my sexual prowess would have been like accepting, night after night, an obscene telephone call collect: heavy breathing, reverse the charges.

His latest communication, however, like a dead mouse in a box of corn pellets, caused my twitch. My brainpower, my sexual prowess, my discretion and my ancestry are one thing, and, of course, problematic. My morals, my character, are another. If pressed, I would say that the only people entitled to criticize them are the women and children in my life, although I wish they wouldn't. But here was this dead mouse, a stranger to me but a figure of some inflation in the salons of power and success, impugning my motives. "Impugning my motives": see how ridiculously quaint, almost campy, that sounds? My dead mouse asserted that I had arrived at an opinion not for the reasons I had explained in the course of arriving at it, but for dark, cheap and sensational purposes of an undisclosed, reprehensible nature.

I found, to my chagrin, that I was angry. I am ulterior on my own time, not the public's. There is, however, nothing one can do with such anger in the modern world, no dustbins in which to deposit it. Mention a duel and the cognoscenti snort. (Actually, snorting is what cognoscenti do best.) Duels didn't do Pushkin, Hamilton or Lermontov any good. As the world turns, I might meet my dead mouse at a cocktail party or a symposium. Ought I then endeavor to cause him to sneeze his teeth? I haven't been in a fist fight since junior high school. I would prefer to read Norman Mailer than to *be* him.

A sense of honor is a waste of emotion.

One calms down, of course. The thermostat of sanity sees to that, along with the exigencies of opinionizing on a deadline. But something curious and valuable is gained in the course of an honorable snit, an accession hard to define. Just as when your own marriage falls apart you suddenly start reading the signs of tension and fatigue and despair in the faces of other couples soon to part, so as you contemplate your vestigial tailbone of honor do you start listening to other people who have clearly "felt a stain like a wound." Other people twitch, too, and don't know what to do about the insult. Because there is no socially acceptable way to avenge the insult, they (we) walk around the block, spit at cats, dream of duels, eventually calm down and are, as a consequence, by a fingernail diminished.

A fingernail counts. Critical discourse has so degenerated that maybe it's impossible for any of us to expect a decent regard of our vagaries of judgment, the sincere blunder. I apologize, not to my dead mouse, but to those faces I failed to read, those signals I failed to receive from friends who were helpless to contain or purge a thoughtless or inadvertent insult to their honor. It occurs to me that if we feel this ferocious guppy swimming in our gut, we might somewhere inside ourselves find vestiges of virtue, a spine, even heart.

The Diet

Inside the house, they were dieting. So I went out to the garden to count the tulips. We planted tulips last October. To my astonishment, they are coming up, one by one, as if they knew exactly how to do it. I am astonished because I am regarded by my many enemies as a Black Thumb; I have merely to enter a room and the vegetable kingdom perishes. Somehow, the tulips hadn't gotten the word.

When dieting goes on, the house is loud. You would think that not eating would be quiet. That's just the trouble. When they diet, they eat *more*, only differently. They have lists of food on which it is permissible to gorge. They argue about exceptions to rules that change each season, about systems as complex as quantum mechanics. This seems to me less a diet than a form of cabalism. I have found them under the coffee table, moaning, up to their wrists in wheels of cheese.

From personal experience, I know that the only way to lose weight is to stop eating. I realize that this system is un-American. Somewhere in the Bill of Rights is a Pig Amendment; our freedom to stuff ourselves cannot be abridged. Having so stuffed, we demand a technological solution for the fat problem. Give me cyclamates, or give me death! This is not only immoral; it is also boring.

Sixteen years ago I gave up smoking for thirty-six months. I was, alas, still in the oral stage. Two things happened: (1) I gained thirty pounds and looked like a toad. (2) I couldn't write. I couldn't write because there was a bowl of potato chips instead of an ashtray beside my electric typewriter. The potato chips made greasy the tips of my fingers, which slid hideously across the keyboard of the typewriter, slamming the carriage back and forth, causing bad puns and much gibberish to spew upon the world. Nobody wants to be a toad who can't write.

And so I turned in my electric typewriter for a manual; I resumed sticking burning leaves into my food hole, and I went on a diet.

A DAY IN THE LIFE OF MY DIET

22 cups of black coffee
½ pound raw meat
3 fingers cheap bourbon whiskey

The advantage of this diet is that the bourbon knocks you out; otherwise, after all that coffee, your bed would feel like an electric chair. This diet also punches holes in the brain, so that the oxygen can leak away. And it works.

In six months I lost forty pounds, my sweet tooth and my will to live. Living was much less interesting than dieting. I spent hours in the bathroom on the scales. Mine was the ecstasy of self-denial; rid of the sin of flab, honed down to a tuning fork of bone, I would, if struck, give off a pitch so perfect that matter itself would shatter and atoms disperse on winds of light. All that was opaque would be transparent.

I am better now, thank you.

Anyway, I was standing in the garden, thinking about self-denial and tulips and looking at the stacks of garbage and sticks of broken furniture behind the restaurant across the way that were looming over my magnolia bush. I have been worried about this garbage. It has been there for months, ever since they closed the restaurant and went off to Phoenix or Nepal to launder their money. At first, I preferred the uncollected garbage to what had preceded it: the louts who staffed the restaurant and would on summer nights at 2 a.m. gather above my magnolia bush for a couple of joints and a fit of giggles and noisy divagations on the sex life of the mollusk. Lately, though, I have wanted to pluck out the eyesore that offends me.

All right. I stood there, and then from somewhere above, like a hawk or a spear, there fell a burning broom. No question about it, this was a broom with its bristles in flames. Its descent was curiously languid. It landed in the garbage in back of the restaurant.

My first thought was the Red Brigades. My next thought was Götterdämmerung. Finally, I remembered the hose, which I dragged the length of the garden in order to squirt at the burning broom in the garbage. I had, however, neglected to remember that I had closed off the water pipe to the outside for the winter. Back, then, into the dieting house, down to the cellar, to do some twisting of knobs. The garden was still there when I returned.

Unfortunately, a leaky linkage between faucet and hose reduced the water pressure to a trickle, while managing to drench me as I tried to repair it. Fortunately, two young men shouting something about "a barbecue that got out of hand" appeared with buckets on the roof of the restaurant and doused the flames. They were too far away to be hit by the invectives I hurled at them.

Now, while I tried to imagine how one sets a broom on fire while trying to cook dinner, the sky began to fall. Not, properly, the sky, but the apartment house next door: wood, plaster, dirt and bricks rushed down the side of the building. The dirt and plaster dust gathered in a cloud floating my way, which adhered to my wet clothes. The bricks bounced off the fire-escape scaffolding and caromed into my garden. I could see workmen, hammering with their backs to me, in the windows of the eighth floor of the apartment house. My hose drooped. Without enough water pressure, I was helpless to retaliate.

I went into the house, up the stairs, to the kitchen. There the dieters were tonguing themselves like cats. "Leg of lamb," they hyperventilated. "Quiche au Roquefort. Tarte aux cerises, flambée. Pringles!"

"They are trying to murder our tulips," I said in a rage, "and all you can think about is your stomach. I give this city tulips, and this city gives back to me a brick and a burning broom. Deny the self and think of the tulips, for pity's sake!"

So they went down into the garden and ate the tulips.

Going to Greece

The last tulip is dead. They were brave, the tulips, for a month, and then their heads fell off, and it seemed that the floor of the garden was littered with bandannas or torn flags or bold emotions. If I could, I would blame the cats, whose laziness is boring. But the cats respected the tulips, and hid among them. For a month, with the cats and the tulips, the garden was full of so much useless beauty that Marx and Freud and Calvin and Schopenhauer and Sartre, inside on the library shelves, whimpered and groaned; their dusty systems were offended.

It is hard to be serious. The children have gathered and soon we shall sneak off to Greece, one of the many places I have never been. Instead of reading about another dusty system, I sit on the porch with Rex Warner's *The Stories of the Greeks* in my lap. Farrar, Straus & Giroux have squeezed Mr. Warner's three volumes of stories into one, just in time to distract me from my proper work. They are, of course, wonderful stories—from Ovid and Homer and Virgil, Euripides and Aeschylus. One turns from them, naturally, to the plays and the *Iliad*, back, really, to the bloody garden where so much of what we have become started us going.

I used to write doggerel. I was older then. For instance:

> *A sudden blow: the great wings beating still*
> *Above the struggling maid. She wrings its neck*
> *And flings it down and steps upon its bill,*
> *And says: "You dirty bird!"*
> > *Après le kill,*
> *She had it stuffed and set it on a shelf . . .*
> *Poor Agamemnon had to stab himself.*

Some rude familiarity with both Greek mythology and the poems of William Butler Yeats is required to appreciate just how much has been trivialized in so few lines. This is a consequence of having grown up better acquainted with the activities of Zeus than with the activities of Jehovah. The gods I cared about from the time I was five years old never seemed to have anything on their minds except sex and pride. Antigone was my kind of sister.

Whenever I take a shower, I think of the Shower of Gold. I never take baths, because of Clytemnestra. My office is Augean.

Westerners probably can't even think without in some sense thinking Greek. Most of our words for most of the important things—chemistry, physics, economics, politics, ethics, aesthetics, theology, tragedy, comedy and so on—were given to us by the Greeks. As I have explained over and over again to my son—my Hector, my Orestes, and not, I hope, my Icarus—Aristotle's table of categories was a sort of Trojan zebra, foisting the unconscious dualisms of Greek grammar upon the unsuspecting cosmos.

Perhaps W. H. Auden was a little clearer on the subject. The Greeks, he said, "have taught us, not to think—that all human beings have always done— but to think about our thinking, to ask such questions as, 'What do I think?,' 'What do this and that other person or people think?,' 'On what do we agree and disagree? Why?' And not only did they learn to ask questions about thinking, but they also discovered how, instead of giving immediate answers, to suppose something to be the case and then see what would follow if it were."

I like that. In Auden's opinion, the Athenians of the fifth century B.C. "were the most civilized people who have so far existed." And I am going to Athens. I am told that the Athens Hilton has a fine view of the Acropolis, but I promised my mother never to stay in a Hilton. I am told that the hotel we will be staying in has a fine view of the Hilton.

If not for Pyramus and Thisbe, how could there have been Romeo and Juliet? If not for Oedipus, how could there have been a complex? Without Homer, life would have been much more difficult for James Joyce. As it is, the Blind Seer is a tradition: Homer, Milton, Joyce, Ray Charles.

My son, of course, is reading the *Aeneid*. One of the reasons I dropped Latin after a single year is that I knew they would make me read the *Aeneid*, in the original, and I believe Virgil to be anal-retentive. Besides, as Thomas Paine pointed out in *The Age of Reason,*

From what we know of the Greeks, it does not appear that they knew or studied any language but their own, and this was one cause of their becoming so learned; it afforded them more time to apply themselves to better studies.

I'm still learning English.

Consider the Minotaur and the labyrinth and Jorge Luis Borges. Without Proserpine, Swinburne would have been impossible, not to mention tulips. Without Orpheus, we would have missed Monteverdi's C major to C sharp: Eurydice is dead. Narcissus and Echo speaks for themselves.

A world without nymphs and Furies and dryads and Atalanta is a world of nothing but highways and sewers, like Rome or Cleveland. Compared with Prometheus, Faust was a twerp, and everybody since Faust has been Dennis the Menace.

I find myself on the porch looking at the garden with the tears of Priam in my eyes. There are bulls and stags and swans and centaurs and Socrates in the garden, with the wind chimes and the severed heads of tulips. I don't have to go to Greece. It is here. It is the furniture of my brain. But I'll go anyway. You don't tell Darius not to try to bridge the Hellespont.

Dolphins

We are about twenty minutes east of Heraklion, on the northern coast of Crete, in a whitewashed bungalow with a veranda at which the Mediterranean laps, a kilometer or two away from an island populated entirely by goats. The stars show off. By the light of the Big Dipper, the female children play backgammon and the male child reads *Zorba the Greek*. The female adult is across the road, buying a bag of peaches and a bottle of wine. The male adult is deep into ouzo and rhapsodizing.

That the male child can read at all is a small amazement. We left the port of Piraeus on the *Ariadne* to Heraklion Sunday afternoon, without having had to sacrifice a member of the family for favorable winds. On board the *Ariadne* were many television sets, so that the World Cup soccer match might be watched. The male adult, instead, paced the deck, looking for dolphins. We docked at six in the morning on Monday. By seven, the children were swimming in the Mediterranean. By eight, before breakfast, the male child had dropped his glasses in the bathroom and smashed a lens.

He had never been abroad before, and suddenly he couldn't see. Like many male children not quite yet sixteen years old, he magnifies his own misfortunes; they assume a teleological significance. He was being punished. Indeed, in Greece, with so much beauty everywhere, it is possible to understand why it was necessary to invent the idea of nemesis. Of what use was a father against nemesis, outside a strange city in a foreign land, unable to speak the language?

He should have known better. The gods were with us. We waited that night on the road for the bus to Heraklion, which never came. But a taxi returning from a drop along the beach slowed down and we clambered in, along with half the Greek Army, clutching our map. Maria, the receptionist at the hotel, had a friend, George, who ran a car-rental agency in Heraklion. George was rumored to know somebody. And there proved to be a George, who made a telephone call and an appointment for eight o'clock that evening. Father and son lolled in an agreeable café. We were led at eight through narrow, winding streets of the Venetian persuasion to an ophthalmologist who flashed numbers, not Greek letters, on the screen. The usual things were said about astigmatism, a prescription was written, eight hundred drachmas changed hands, George disappeared with the prescription and the manager of our hotel, who just happened to be waiting around at the car-rental agency, drove us back to our bungalow.

George delivered the glasses to the hotel the next day, refusing all forms of emolument. George, I now know, could have found us a witch doctor or a translation into Urdu of Linear A, had we needed either one. But I am content to let my son believe that his father is the sort of person who consorts as an equal with the Georges of this world.

The matter of the broken glasses released us from our feeble cautions, our wary twitching. We ought to have known that everything in Greece would be wonderful except the coffee, the caryatids and the Germans. We were such ambulatory advertisements of the will to believe, the need to sigh, to listen to the stones sing at Delphi and Mycenae, to watch the great tragedies on the mountain stage at Epidaurus. How could they have let us down? It would have been rude. And so they arranged for the oleanders and the olive trees and the watermelon, the bronze charioteer and the tomb of Agamemnon, the labyrinth and the volcano and George.

Did we desire to eat something else besides souvlaki and moussaka in Athens? There were grocery stores and kiosks. And three blocks away from the Golden Age (!) Hotel was, obligingly, a taverna called Othello's, run by a Greek Cypriot who loved Shakespeare and was ambivalent about the English. His establishment was empty because he refused to have a television set, even for the World Cup. He prepared delicious hamburgers for the children; I was mortified. But we bought each other Metaxa brandies, and discussed Desdemona, and the children went forth like goats hungry for sensations, drunk on beauty, to touch the omphalos; to walk on the plain of Argos; to petition Poseidon; to anchor themselves against the fierce wind blowing from the Gorge of the Dead on the way to Zakros; to swim in the shadow of the Matala caves, a hundred and thirty miles from the coast of Africa. In his prowl about the Minoan palace at Knossos, my son, my Theseus, found a bullring, and saw—through a perfectly satisfactory new pair of glasses—a snake.

We were not misled by the books and our imagination. The Parthenon, once you have hacked your way through thickets of Germans, is not overrated, even though it breathes in isolation from a city very much like Pittsburgh, in suspended time. I talked to Socrates in the agora, and he was hard on my case. The Minoans, I was told, were only four and a half feet tall; they had to stand on footstools to get into their own ornamental vases and jars. I should be so big, so busy making beauty before the next earthquake or the next Turk.

We are ready now to island-hop, a family of five, inconvenient in restaurants and taxicabs, with no reservations anywhere, not even in our minds: Santorini, Naxos, Paros, Mykonos and—that boneyard of antiquities—Delos, where Apollo was born and took his winter vacations. We will dare to eat a peach. We all wear new glasses from the third millennium before Christ. We have internalized George.

I explain to my son on the veranda that monotheism was a terrible idea, leading directly to Lenin. He isn't interested.

I complain to my son that I haven't seen a dolphin. He is surprised. I study his face, and those of his sisters. *They* have seen dolphins, everywhere. I am, as usual, sincere but wrong. They *are* dolphins, swimmers in our dream and my ouzo.

It and Who

The story begins in a taverna outside Athens on a Saturday night. It will, I hope, never end, but if it is merely an anecdote, the punch line came ten days later in Santorini, the southernmost of the Cycladic islands and, in my opinion, the most beautiful place in the world, where the pure light burns straight through your skull and falls like a sword a thousand feet into the sea.

That night in Athens we were dinner guests of people who had been lucky enough to be assigned to Greece by *The New York Times*. They were briefing us. I was watching my son eat. My son is notorious on both coasts of the United States as a picky eater. He chews no strangeness. And yet, after five days of love among the ruins, there he sat with his mouth open. Into that mouth went three helpings of Iranian caviar on toast, two plates of fried zucchini, green peppers with sausage and a main course of wild boar and celery stew.

I should have known then that he was going native. But he was also listening. Our hosts reported, with some humor, the way the Athens Hilton tries to explain to American tourists how to say "thank you" in Greek. "Thank you" in Greek sounds like "ehfkhahreesto." The Athens Hilton suggests thinking of the phrase as a name: "F. Harry Stowe." This information was consumed along with the wild boar and the fried zucchini.

He had, then, a week in Crete before invading the Cyclades. We practiced living on our own schedule. We learned to saunter. We ate at midnight. The children assumed what would prove to be their characteristic personalities as travelers. My son was a knowledgeable goat. On being forced out of bed to visit yet another palace or temple, he would climb to the highest point of the terrain and brood, eating beauty. One of his sisters was a Roman, in a rage to see and do everything, wearing herself out by making too many appointments with the mysteries. The other sister was emphatically Greek; her genius was a gift of harmony and scale, for being in season. Hers was the rhythm we sought to approximate, with each day of self-improvement followed by a day of self-indulgence.

This was an excellent preparation for the islands. On achieving an island, we would park the duffel bags and the children at an outdoor café, leave them to order whatever squeeze of lemon they thought would quench their thirst and saunter around town looking for appropriate lodging. There is no need to hurry when there is no chance for a mistake. It was possible on Paros, for example, to ride donkeys into the mountains to visit the Garden of the Butterflies, to ride back again with flowers and, if I am not mistaken, leaves of marijuana, to stop for beer on the beach while the children swam in the Aegean, to dry off, to wander twenty or thirty yards, to find a splendid taverna and to eat-squid, without ever looking at a watch. The sun was our watch.

But I must speak of Santorini. It is the rim of a volcano, the very volcano whose eruption is rumored to have wiped out the Minoan civilization and to have sunk Atlantis. I would like to believe this rumor. Phira, a white-and-blue-washed town, sits on the top of the cliff. The only way up from the sea is by donkey. I am sorry I had to come down. It is not the site of interesting ruins, nor are there distinguished beaches, although you can go by motorboat to the sulfurous crust, the "fried rocks" of the Great Kaimeni, and wonder whether Plato had his story straight. Nor, I was told by swingers, is the disco action much to brag or sweat about. I do not, however, swing. Santorini simply abides in its modulations of light, its sheer perspectives, its steep art. It attaches wings to the eyes, and they fly and falter and drown in colors.

My son, of course, disappeared to climb, and was found an hour or two later at the top of the world, looking at Turkey. Or so I thought. He was actually, he told me, thinking about "It." All of It. I didn't need to ask what It was, although I admit to some envy. He was young enough, after thinking about It, to do something about It; I was along for the ride. And the top of the world was a fine place to do one's thinking because in Phira proper, in the middle of the afternoon, the boats disgorge, the donkeys are boarded, the tourists ascend and everybody has two hours to buy. A fever of credit cards obtains. We watched along with a goat. Down there somewhere, his sisters were also buying, and taking photographs. No more than I swing do I buy, except for my stomach, or take photographs, having no need to prove to anybody else that I've been where I was. Buying and snapshots, my son and I agreed, weren't It.

Still, the following afternoon my son was there on a narrow street for the two-hour raid of the tourists. One, a huge American wearing a Stetson and speaking Sunbelt, examined a trinket. He turned to my shaggy son and asked, "How much?" My amazed son looked at the perfectly obvious tag on the trinket and said, "One hundred drachmas." The Stetson nodded, thought about it and then said slowly, carefully, enunciating every syllable: "F. Harry Stowe." My son is not altogether solemn. After a pause, he replied: "Who?"

Well, that is indeed the question when we travel, and a hard one. The Stetson complained, "You're not Greek!" The Stetson was wrong. My son, briefly, *was* Greek, almost Aristophanic. Who and It are the big imponderables, for explanations of which we do not go to the Hilton or buy worry beads or take snapshots. We saunter and climb and brood and shake sticks at trees and clouds of butterflies. If It is more than we can know, Who is enough to be, so long as we are willing to eat wild boar and beauty.

I will settle for being the father who took his children to Greece while their eyes were still innocent and their ears heard music.

The Caryatid

This was before the air conditioner dropped out of the ninth-floor window of a nearby apartment house, bounced off the roof of the seedy disco and ricocheted into my garden. It was before my newspaper took away all our typewriters, took away all our noise and gave us machines with ghosts in them, machines that watch us while we try to write. It was before Billy Martin and Peter Bourne and Christina Onassis and the test-tube baby and the inscrutable yen. It was, in other words, back in the days, just a few weeks ago, when I thought I could cope.

I had plenty of time to think. Our T.W.A. charter flight from Athens, after a pit stop in Paris, landed at Kennedy Airport without any luggage. Or so it seemed as the hours limped by and the children fell, like stunned deer, down to the dirty floor. There is not, between passport control and the stables of customs, a place to sit, nor anything to eat or drink. Outside, I knew, the imperial city was waiting. And my underwear was in Paris or Helsinki.

I would like to think that we had been visitors, not tourists. But we had been tourists. We went where tourists go. Why not? Where tourists go, there is usually something to see. This is one of the agreeable mysteries of life, like the tendency of famous men to be born on holidays. And it is easier to be a tourist in Greece than in most other places because of the scale.

It is, of course, a balanced scale. Art, or nature, is on one side, and man is on the other, and the proportions are right. Between man and nature, between man and art, there is a Meaningful Relationship. Even Mount Parnassus lacks hubris, and is satisfied to rise less than half as high as Mount McKinley, less than a third as high as Everest. Nor would it have occurred to the Greeks to carve a huge face of, say, Pericles on the side of Mount Parnassus. My objection, in fact, to caryatids is that they violate the scale. In his wonderful book *Classical Landscape with Figures*, Osbert Lancaster asked,

How could the Greeks with their clear, logical outlook and their unshakably humanistic standards of taste ever have tolerated, let alone evolved, the caryatid? . . . At the [Acropolis] these elegant flowermaidens simper as unconcernedly as if they had never been called upon to balance the two and a half tons of Pentelic marble on their pretty little heads.

I digress. It may be that the Greeks had it easy, with their light and their mountains and their plains and their islands waiting around for tourists. It was easy for them to believe that man fit in rather well. This fittingness might have given them the idea that we are seemlier than other evidence suggests. The heads of Rameses II at Abu Simbel and, for that matter, the skyscrapers of New York, have another idea of man. So do the artifacts of Albert Speer. It is depressing to wonder whether the Greeks just happened to be lucky, and the dream they left us is a lie about ourselves.

But if we were tourists, we were not without honor. We learned quickly. Among the things we learned is that not every transaction between tourist and native is a business deal. The man who picked up a family of five on the road and dropped us half an hour later at a museum spoke less English than we did Greek, but managed to make himself clear when I offered him money. "I am not a taxi," he said. "I am . . . what? I am *souvenir*." He smiled. I bought us a cup of coffee. We tried to talk in French. The scale was just right. I see now that, as tourists, we were acquisitive. We were, however, buying emotions, or being given them. We became fiercely possessive of our Greece, as if the moments and the light were shards of Mycenae, bone splinters of dead kings. Either that sense of possession inspired many human kindnesses, or the kindnesses were simply there, available as a matter of course to strangers, like the beauty.

And so we seemed to have gone to a different Greece from the one that had annoyed the people around us on the charter flight back from Athens. I couldn't recognize my Greece in their complaints. They complained about the food and the heat and the accommodations and the language, quite as if a country were not entitled to its own cuisine and weather and words, as if the entire world is obliged to be a Howard Johnson's restaurant and a Holiday Inn. I would have thought it impossible not to enjoy Greece, unless you never got out of the hotel dining room or the air-conditioned tour bus. My children had to be restrained from doing bodily harm to the bad-mouthers. The bad-mouthers cheered when we touched down at Kennedy. "Thank God," said the woman behind me, "I'm finally someplace where they understand me." No, you're not, lady. No wonder the luggage wasn't there. They didn't deserve their luggage. They deserved to miss their connecting flight to Miami, and I am happy to report that they missed it.

All right, then. It was necessary to reacquaint ourselves with the scale of our city. Our duffel bags went unmolested by customs. At the exit a local poltroon sized up the five of us. "Taxi," he said. Yeah, we said. Forty dollars for a limousine to Manhattan, he said. Forget it, we said. Forty dollars is neither a taxi nor a souvenir. You'll never get a cab for five people, he said. Never, never, never—as he followed us down the street, furious. "Listen, buster," said my wife, "I *live* in this city. Shove off."

Shove off? My wife said shove off? She also snapped her gum. We achieved a Checker. If we could cope with Greece, we could cope with New York, but the scale was different. And I sit here, talking to the ghost in my machine, and why—at home, where air conditioners fall out of the sky in the middle of the night and pillheads occupy the White House—do I still feel like a tourist, or a caryatid?

A NOTE ON THE TYPE

The text of this book was set in Caledonia, a Linotype face designed by W. A. Dwiggins. It belongs to the family of printing types called "modern face" by printers—a term used to mark the change in style of type letters that occurred in about 1800. Caledonia borders on the general design of Scotch Modern, but is more freely drawn than that letter.

Composed by Maryland Linotype Composition Company, Inc., Baltimore, Maryland. Printed and bound by The Haddon Craftsmen, Inc., Scranton, Pennsylvania